JEREMY PANG'S CHINESE KITCHEN

SCHOOL OF WOK

JEREMY PANG'S
CHINESE KITCHEN

SCHOOL OF WOK

**SIMPLE TECHNIQUES.
DELICIOUS RECIPES.**

FOREWORD 6
INTRODUCTION 7
CHINESE KITCHEN ESSENTIALS 10
SEASONING & MAINTAINING YOUR WOK 14
OTHER EQUIPMENT 16
PREPARATION TECHNIQUES 17
THE CHINESE PANTRY 22
THE WOK CLOCK 42
BALANCE IN CHINESE FOOD 43

CHAPTER 1
STIR-FRYING 44

CHAPTER 2
DEEP-FRYING 76

CHAPTER 3
STEAMING 106

CHAPTER 4
POACHING & BRAISING 138

CHAPTER 5
ROASTING & DOUBLE-COOKING 166

CHAPTER 6
SALADS, PICKLES & SIDES 192

GLOSSARY 215
INDEX 216
ACKNOWLEDGEMENTS 223

FOREWORD

In my 50 years of writing and teaching Chinese cookery in books, in classes and on television, I have always valued its cooking techniques, the history of Chinese ingredients and showing my audience how they can duplicate what I have shared with them. My goal was that they would have a fundamental understanding and appreciation of one of the most ancient cuisines in the world.

Today in this book, Jeremy Pang has successfully distilled the essence of how to make delicious authentic Chinese dishes through simply explained clear techniques. No doubt, having an acclaimed cookery school has given him the experience of teaching novices how to cook. Every essential aspect is carefully explained with a sense of humour; Jeremy's voice comes through clear and strong. Each recipe is written with simple instructions on how to prepare and cook each dish. Possible substitutions, or 'swapsies', are helpful as well and there are some great tips, as if Jeremy was right beside you.

His notes infuse the entire book with personal experiences, observations and wit that make cooking fun. I also love how some of the recipes have been given new life with unusual ingredients, sauces and a very British touch. The magnificent instructional and mouth-watering photos bring each offering to life and are sure to make any reader run into the kitchen to try many of them.

This book is not only for aspiring chefs but also for anybody interested in cooking. I am certain you will find it as enlightening as I did and will agree that it belongs in any serious cook's kitchen and their cookery library.

KEN HOM CBE

CHEF, BBC-TV PRESENTER & AUTHOR
BANGKOK, THAILAND
APRIL, 2025

INTRODUCTION

We Chinese have a knack of keeping our cooking a secret. It's almost as if, when the Chinese first started migrating across the world, we held a cultural pact – a unanimous understanding that we should open Chinese restaurants, perhaps, but never give away any of the secrets of Chinese cooking. I suppose it makes sense. After all, we would only be giving our restaurants competition if we did so…

Almost ten years ago I wrote my first cookbook, *Chinese Unchopped*, but to be honest, at the time I had no idea I was able to write anything worthy of an audience and I was still working out the ins and outs of adult life. I was just turned 30, newly married and every penny I owned was invested into this crazy idea of mine to open an Asian cookery school in the heart of Central London. A decade later, I realize that the idea of School of Wok wasn't crazy at all, and that there are hundreds of thousands of people out there who share the very same inquisitive passion for Chinese cuisine as I do. It's down to your belief, and following that self-belief I'm here today rewriting the book that got us all so excited about Chinese food in the first place. For those of you who were lucky enough to get your hands on a copy of *Chinese Unchopped* before it went completely out of print, here's a blast from the past but with plenty more recipes and ten more years of learning and added practical tips on how to get to grips with all the secrets of Chinese home cooking.

Although my dad was a brilliant cook and inspired my love for food, he flatly refused to teach me his 'Chinese kitchen secrets'. Rather, he would insist we children sat and watched while he skipped across the kitchen and got to work. Twenty minutes later (and far too fast for us to work out what had happened), dinner would be on the table. After a few minutes of silent scoffing, he would make us guess exactly what he had put into each dish. Although we would be none the wiser as to how dinner was made, this daily palate training kept our taste buds constantly excited and has definitely led me to where I am today. Unlike my dad, though, I am here to tell you all my kitchen secrets.

Being British-born Chinese, I've been lucky enough to experience and enjoy the wonders of both cultures and, while my Chinese language skills are terrible to say the least, I am proud to say I've retained a crucial part of my Chinese cultural identity – a love of eating and cooking. Truth be told I was a little fearful that that my ambition would be frowned upon

by almost all the Chinese restaurateurs in the country. A Chinese cookery school certainly wasn't part of the unspoken arrangement our families and ancestors all seemed to have made! However, it's now clear to me that the two aren't mutually exclusive – there are times when you want to eat at home and others when you just don't.

Chinese food really isn't as daunting to cook as it may at first seem. Like any cuisine, when examined closely and from a basic level, the patterns and techniques it follows quickly become obvious. In the last 15 years – teaching in completely different environments and with all different types of hobs, heat, woks and knives – I have learned more about Chinese cookery than ever before, and it is through these experiences that I have come to understand its core cooking techniques. Some of these techniques may take a little patience and practice to get the hang of at first (but doesn't anything worth learning?), but once mastered, they will give you the confidence to create an amazing repertoire of Chinese dishes in any home kitchen environment.

The aim of this refreshed version of *Chinese Unchopped* is to help further unravel the wonders of our once-guarded Chinese kitchen secrets and demystify the core techniques of Chinese cooking to get you cooking and eating perhaps the best Chinese food you have ever eaten at home. Whether you want a simple one-wok wonder with a bowl of rice on the side or are feeling brave enough to cook three or four dishes to create a feast to impress your friends and family, through my recipes, descriptions and instructions, I hope to be able to help you achieve a wonderful Chinese home-cooking experience.

CHINESE KITCHEN ESSENTIALS

I often joke about turning up at university with a wok and a big bag of rice, but with these two Chinese kitchen essentials, you will never go hungry. The wok is a far more versatile kitchen tool than a toastie machine, and understanding how to use one automatically leads to a healthier lifestyle.

THE CLEAVER

What is the difference between a Chinese cleaver and a Chinese chopper? Are they the same thing? Are they just big Western butchers' knives with Chinese writing on them? Do I really need one to cook Chinese food?

Well, none of these statements is necessarily correct. Much like Western and Japanese chefs' knives, there are hundreds of different types of cleavers (a composite term) that have various uses within the Chinese cooking world. And while no, you don't necessarily need one to make Chinese food, they are an interesting and efficient piece of equipment to have and enjoy should you decide to make the purchase. They come with their own history and their own specific technique, different from the Western knife, making them a unique and useful addition to your kitchen equipment.

Cleavers come in many different shapes, sizes, thicknesses and weights – from general slicers to duck slicers (a knife closer in size to a Japanese *santoku*, but again with less weight on top of the blade than the Japanese equivalents), and general choppers to *kau kong* (heavyweight choppers). There are even cleavers made specially to create perfectly round dim sum pastries. The difference between a cleaver and a chopper is the weight of the knife itself and the material it is designed to cut through.

For those looking to make their first cleaver purchase, I would recommend starting with a general slicer or what we call our 'slice and dice cleaver' at School of Wok. General slicers tend to have a nice thin blade, with a well-balanced weight and a good-sized handle that is comfortable to grip. These types of cleavers are designed for slicing and simple vegetable chopping, but not for chopping through bones. If you want to chop through bones, it's best to leave that to a butcher, or invest in a chopper – a cleaver specifically made with enough weight and thickness on the top of the blade to withstand the extra force required to cut through tougher material without breaking the thin blade. Bone-in eating in Chinese cuisine is something that may take getting used to for some, but we are big believers in meat staying more succulent when left on the bone. The recipe for Yong Ping Yellow Chicken on page 164, for example, calls for chopped-up whole chicken legs complete with skin and bone to make the chicken more bite-sized while maintaining its succulence throughout the cooking process.

When it comes to using your cleaver, efficiency is key. Slicing is by far the most efficient way of prepping your food. A good slicer has an incredibly sharp, thin blade with only a slightly thicker top edge giving balance to the knife.

The instinct for anyone new to a cleaver is to pick it up and use a classic up-and-down chopping motion. Descriptions of techniques and names of dishes in Chinese cuisine are quite literal, and with cleavers it's no different, so depending on whether you have chosen a general slicer, duck slicer or *kau kong* chopper, the chopper will chop, whereas the slicers will slice, with great precision as long as you practise your technique! (See pages 18–21 for slicing and dicing tips and tricks.)

THE WOK

Back in the old days, woks used to be made completely out of cast iron with a handle on either side of the wok bowl that would heat up just as much as the wok itself. Even the thinner versions would be extremely heavy to handle. These cast-iron woks are still available and feel wonderful to use, but I would never attempt to flick a cast-iron wok. Instead, I reserve them for slower-cooked braised dishes or deep-frying, as they retain their heat incredibly well.

The best modern-day stir-frying woks are made of thin carbon steel. They conduct heat incredibly well, but more importantly, due to the thin metal, they also lose heat very quickly, which suits stir-frying perfectly, as the quick change in the temperature of the pan allows you to control the level of heat, creating smoking-hot heat when needed, and also to circulate the heat around the wok, which in Cantonese we call having good *wok hei*, or 'wok's air'. This process of quick-searing or blistering the ingredients before pushing them to the side of the wok or manoeuvring them with a flick, toss or a quick stir retains the texture of the ingredients and also seals a unique smoky flavour into the food.

Mastering the art of *wok hei* is key to any stir-fry and is unique to wok cooking. If you were a fly on the wall at a traditional Chinese restaurant, it would be unusual not to hear a conversation between friends about whether the wok chef has good *wok hei* or not. One who has the natural ability to know when to circulate the right level of heat around the wok can impart the perfect amount of smoke to the ingredients while maintaining their natural sweetness, texture and aroma, before pouring the whole dish, sizzling hot, out of the wok ready to devour. In fact, *wok hei* is the main reason why Chinese food is never great when delivered and is always best eaten freshly cooked.

The starting point to perfecting your *wok hei* is picking the right wok; the larger the surface area of the wok, the more ingredients you can put in. Traditional woks are round-based, because the circular bowl assists the circulation of heat around the pan, which is essential for stir-frying or tossing ingredients and for *wok hei*. However, round-based woks are best used on a gas hob, so if you have an electric or induction hob, I would recommend opting for a flat-based wok instead. While there are plenty of flat-based woks on the market, my best tip is to look for one that has some good curvature and a smooth bowl shape even though it has a flat base, so that you can still achieve that all-important circular movement for good *wok hei*. (See pages 48–9 for more details and advice on how to supercharge your stir-frying skills.)

Nonstick woks were invented for easy cleaning and have the benefit of simple maintenance. Although not as hard-wearing as traditional carbon-steel woks, newer models are increasingly resistant to damage from everyday use and utensils Personally, I still much prefer to use the traditional carbon-steel woks and cast-iron woks; they give off that extra smoky, caramelized stir-fry flavour when cooking. So, if you really want to get your stir-fries closer to those of your favourite Chinese restaurants and takeaways (if not better), then get yourself a carbon-steel wok and take the time when you first buy it to season it (see page 14). You can now also buy pre-seasoned carbon-steel woks. These are fully black and look like nonstick woks, but they are seasoned in the factory to save you having to season it at home. They are, however, still made of carbon steel, so it's crucial not to skip the cleaning and drying process as explained on page 15, to maintain their condition and avoid any corrosion.

SEASONING & MAINTAINING YOUR WOK

Most carbon-steel woks will come with an anti-rust layer to prevent them from corroding when sitting on a shop shelf, but seasoning a carbon-steel wok, as below, is essential to creating a natural nonstick surface on the wok. If your wok later develops any spots of rust, repeat the seasoning steps below. Look after your wok, and it should last a lifetime!

CREATING A NATURAL NONSTICK LAYER

1

Give the wok a good scrub with a metal scourer.

2

Heat the wok over a high gas flame until the inside is a dark grey/blue colour all the way around. Then remove it from the heat and let the wok cool down.

3

Dip a thick pad of kitchen towel in a little vegetable oil and use it to polish the inside of the wok by rubbing it all over the wok in a circular motion.

4

Heat the wok over a high heat until it starts to smoke. Once all the smoke disappears and the wok is dark grey/black in colour it is ready to use.

KEEPING YOUR WOK CLEAN & SEASONED

1

To clean the wok, half-fill it with hot water and place it over a high heat.

2

Boil the water vigorously and de-glaze the wok.

3

Clean the wok thoroughly with hot water and a sponge or metal scourer, using a little detergent if necessary.

4

Always dry the wok on the hob over a high heat until all the water has evaporated. Then allow it to cool before putting it away. You should not have to apply any oil to the wok to store it.

OTHER EQUIPMENT

The following equipment and accessories are also incredibly helpful when cooking Chinese food at home and are now easily accessible online. All these ultra-hard-working items of kit come in different shapes and sizes, depending on what suits your requirements best.

WOK LADLES

If you want to get serious with your wok cooking, certain accessories help. Wok ladles, much like Western ladles, are made to hold a certain amount of liquid in the bowl of the spoon. The end of the spoon, however, is positioned at a slightly more obtuse angle to allow for easy stirring and to maintain a good circular movement when it meets a wok full of ingredients.

WOK SPATULA/FISH SLICE

Full metal spatulas can also be found with a similar angle to the wok ladle. They are ideal for when you want to get completely underneath your ingredients without breaking them apart. Some people find spatulas or fish slices easier to use than ladles when folding through food, as they allow the ingredients to be more delicately handled and flicked around the wok.

BAMBOO MESH STRAINERS

What I like to call 'bamboo spiders', these are giant, flat sieves with a large, web-like metal mesh surface and long bamboo handle. Similar to a slotted spoon, these are used to fish out food from a wok or pan when deep-frying or blanching ingredients, but the metal mesh drains the oil or water much more efficiently than a slotted spoon.

COOKING CHOPSTICKS

Wooden cooking chopsticks are so useful and versatile when cooking Chinese food. They essentially act as wooden tongs, but can also be used to test the heat of cooking oil when deep-frying (see page 81). Large wooden chopsticks are especially good for deep-frying, as the extra length keeps you further away from the hot oil in case of spitting. A word of caution: if you want to fish out ingredients from hot oil with cooking chopsticks, please be sure you are confident in using the chopsticks first!

STEAMERS

Steamers come in several different forms, from stainless-steel bases with glass or metal lids to the more traditional bamboo steamers. The other option for steaming, mainly used in the recipes in this book, is to use a large wok with a stainless-steel steamer stand (or shallow heatproof bowl) that fits inside, with a domed lid covering the wok (see below). (See pages 110–11 for more detailed advice on steaming.)

BAMBOO STEAMER BASKET With a bamboo steamer basket as compared to a stainless-steel steamer (see below), the bamboo lid of the steamer collects condensation between the layers of bamboo, acting as a sponge and preventing any water droplets forming on the inside of the lid and dripping back down onto the food.

STAINLESS-STEEL STEAMER This usually comes with a large saucepan at the bottom to hold large amounts of water and therefore it can steam food for longer periods of time, and has a glass or metal lid. If you have a stainless-steel steamer and are worried about condensation and dripping from the lid, the trick is to wrap the lid with a clean tea towel to absorb any excess moisture.

WOK LIDS

The biggest difference between wok cooking versus cooking with a standard frying pan is the increased surface area and volume of food that a wok can hold. The bowl of a wok creates a large surface area to spread food out vertically as well as horizontally and wok lids follow the same principle. The domed shape of a wok lid allows more space for steam to whirl around the wok when covering to steam food through quickly when stir-frying or if you are steaming large ingredients, such as a whole fish or whole chicken and you need that extra height.

PREPARATION TECHNIQUES

Chinese cooking terms are in general much less technical than those of classical Western cooking where, for example, julienne, brunoise and macedoine denote specific types of cuts, but the principles of slicing, dicing, cutting matchsticks and general preparation are just as important in this type of cuisine – if not more so.

Our terms of cooking are instead very literal. When we want something finely sliced, we say it's finely sliced, cut into fine slices. When we need it in big chunks, we cut off a big chunk and check the shape and size with our peers. And when it comes to cooking processes, we call a stir-fry a stir-fry because stirring the food while it fries creates an effective circulation of heat (done in the right way, of course – see pages 48–9 for tips and techniques). Majoring on such a quick-cooking approach, Chinese cooking can as a rule of thumb be split into 90 per cent preparation, 10 per cent cooking. And with such an emphasis on preparation, it's crucial to understand how to use your cleaver properly to slice, dice or chop in the most efficient way possible, as the success of your dish is reliant on this basic preparation of ingredients. We generally slice and dice a lot of our ingredients for two main reasons: in order to cook quickly and so that a little goes a long way and feeds more people, as Chinese food is made to be shared.

Preparation is the key to unlocking successful Chinese cooking. When I am at home cooking a meal for my friends and family, my first step is to prepare all the key ingredients for the meal and set up my Wok Clock (see page 42), beginning with the basic ingredients – ginger, garlic and spring onions or onions. Once everything has been sliced and diced, I then organize myself and get ready to cook, starting with the slowest cooking techniques (roasting, braising and poaching), while leaving the quicker cooking methods (stir-frying, deep-frying and steaming) to the last 15–20 minutes before serving.

Additionally, when considering the different cuts, shapes or sizes, keep in mind that everything you prepare for one dish should be a similar size in order to cook quickly and maintain the texture of the ingredients. Here are some tips on how to improve your general cleaver skills and therefore become much quicker at cooking your home Chinese meals. In fact, if you master these preparation techniques with your cleaver, you will make leaps and bounds in cooking anything, no matter what the cuisine.

A CRASH COURSE IN CLEAVER SKILLS

THE 'CRAB'

Gaining confidence in cleaver skills is down to practice. The non-dominant hand is a 'five-legged crab', with the three middle fingers as the front legs and the thumb and little finger as the back. The golden rule? Never allow the back legs to stray to the front!

1

The hand is crab-like, as the fingers are always bent, never straight. This creates a stable guide for the dominant hand to start slicing.

2

Slightly tuck in the tips of the middle fingers so the top knuckles protrude slightly. Place the side of the cleaver blade against the bent knuckles to be guided by them accordingly.

3

Lift the wrist of your cleaver hand, with the tip of the blade on the surface or, if your ingredients are standing tall, lift the whole blade up to allow enough space for your cleaver blade to touch the top of the ingredients. Always keep the tip of the blade at least 1–2cm (½–¾ inch) ahead of what you are slicing.

4

Use long, stroking movements in a down and forwards motion, pushing the blade all the way down to the chopping board. Once the blade is completely flush with the surface of the board, push forwards and slice. Repeat the movement from step 3 and keep slicing in a slow but continuous motion.

SLICING & DICING

Whether slicing, cutting matchsticks or dicing, the closer you manage to hold your blade against the bent knuckles of the front legs (middle fingers) of your crab hand, the finer you will eventually be able to slice and dice your ingredients. If ingredients stick to the blade of your cleaver, push them away from the blade with one finger in a confident, swift motion, allowing them to slip off safely.

SLICES

Present the crab (your non-dominant hand) lightly on top of and in the middle of the ingredients you wish to cut. Push down and forwards with the cleaver to cut a straight edge out of whatever you are cutting. Then place the straight edge down flush with the chopping board and start to slice through the ingredients to the desired thickness, pushing down and forwards, then lifting your wrist and blade for a continuous movement.

MATCHSTICKS

Take your prepared slices and lay them flat on the chopping board, spread out in a uniform line rather than piled up. Using a down and forwards rocking motion, lift up your wrist while pulling back slightly and then push down and forwards and repeat to slice the ingredients into long matchsticks.

DICE

Take your prepared matchsticks and turn them 90 degrees. Using the same rocking motion, start by pushing down and forwards and then, pick up your wrist, repeat the motion and cut the sticks into dice.

THE SCOOP

The beauty of using a cleaver is its large surface area, perfect for picking up lots of ingredients once sliced or diced. To do this safely, take note of the thumb position on my cleaver hand, pushing down hard on top of the blade to ensure the actual blade is sitting flush with the board, and no gap between the board or blade that could allow accidents to happen. Keeping the blade tight to the board with this thumb, scoop the ingredients onto the blade with your crab hand.

MEAT-SLICING TECHNIQUES

CHUNKS

Hold onto the piece of meat with the back legs (thumb and little finger) of your crab on the side of the meat and the front legs (middle fingers) of your crab in a straight line on top of the meat. Using long sawing motions with your cleaver hand, cut the meat into rough chunks.

STRIPS

Fine strips are the quickest and simplest way to cut into your meat for easy stir-fries. Hold onto the piece of meat with your crab hand as when cutting into chunks (see above) and slice into strips no more than 2–3mm (1/16–1/8 inch) thick.

FLATTENED SLICES

After learning the safety of the crab technique, this way of slicing is perhaps a little counter-intuitive and a more advanced lesson in cleaver skills. Carefully lay your crab hand over the meat. Place the blade of your cleaver at a slight angle, roughly 3–4mm (about 1/8 inch) away from the edge of the meat, then slice through the meat on the diagonal in long, slicing and sawing motions. Once you have sliced all the pieces, flatten them with the side of the cleaver to tenderize the meat and create the perfect flattened slices (with a thin but large surface area) for a stir-fry.

HOW TO INFUSE FLAVOUR INTO MEATS

There are plenty of ways to infuse more flavour into meats. This method creates extra surface area across a piece of meat without the need for accessories, such as meat hammers.

1

Place the meat in the centre of your chopping board. Hold the tip of your cleaver with your crab hand.

2

Rock the cleaver up and down in a fast rocking motion and run the blade up and down the piece of meat lightly, taking care not to cut completely through it. This will make lots of little cuts across the meat, opening up the surface area to allow as much of the marinade to penetrate as possible.

3

Once you have made plenty of scores across the meat, slice into whatever shape you desire and then flatten with the side of the cleaver before marinating.

BUTTERFLYING

The large surface area of a cleaver is easy to lay horizontally on top of a piece of meat and slice through to butterfly. This technique can also be applied to slicing and filleting fish smoothly.

1

Lay the side of the cleaver on the centre of your piece of meat, with the bottom of the blade in contact with the meat first. Push the thumb on your cleaver hand down firmly to create a slight groove. Now lightly lay your crab hand on top of the other side. In one slow, long, slicing movement, pulling the cleaver blade towards your torso, slice along the groove down towards you, keeping your cleaver in the horizontal position to cut into the meat while keeping it in one piece.

2

Once you have made the first slice, move your crab hand and pick up the top part of the meat that has just been sliced into. Place your cleaver back into the groove and repeat step 1, but this time pull the meat upwards with your crab hand while you are slicing into the groove. You will see the meat starting to unravel or 'butterfly'. Continue to slice through the groove, pulling upwards, until you have reached the end of the meat, but don't cut through it.

3

Turn your piece of meat over and repeat steps 1–2 on the other side of the meat to open it up fully and finish off the butterflying movement.

THE CHINESE PANTRY

Having a well-stocked pantry is paramount to learning about any new cuisine. Aside from all the wonderful implements and utensils, such as woks or cleavers, I've always thought that the modern Chinese pantry shows just how versatile our cuisine can be. With its use of fermented soybean-based sauces, flavoured oils and China's long history of noodle making, rice agriculture and food preservation, there is a world of store-cupboard ingredients out there.

The problem with such a huge choice of ingredients is that it can become a little daunting. As I'm a big believer in starting small and building onwards and upwards, I would like to touch on just a few store-cupboard ingredients at a time, and by no means should all these pantry items be seen as a necessity to cook Chinese food at home. The basics will serve you just fine.

LEVEL 1 INGREDIENTS

These form the basic level of Chinese pantry that I believe is essential to our cuisine. Once you understand where these ingredients come from and the general principles of how they are used, you will notice that many recipes feature these same simple base ingredients but in differing quantities or they are added at different stages to create layers of flavour. These ingredients are now more often than not found in most Western supermarkets and convenience stores.

Suggested recipes for Level 1 ingredient use: Egg-fried Rice (see page 50); Trout with Chilli Bean, Garlic & Ginger Oil (see page 128); Barbecued Hoisin & Cola Ribs (see page 183).

LEVEL 2 INGREDIENTS

These more obscure ingredients delve further into the realms of Chinese cooking and should start to give you more of an idea of unique Chinese flavours and textures. They may be easier to find in more specialist Asian supermarkets or convenience stores than in Western supermarkets.

Suggested recipes for Level 2 ingredient use: Flash-fried Cabbage with Dried Chillies & Sweetened Soy (see page 56); Curried Squid (page 148); Pickled Lotus Root & Spinach (see page 206).

'SWAPSIES'

Throughout this book, there are suggested 'swapsies', or alternatives, for certain more unusual ingredients for those occasions or situations when they are not at hand or easily found. Although these ingredients will make your food taste closer to the authentic flavours of Chinese cuisine, the true essence of Chinese food is in understanding the core techniques, as set out in each chapter of the book. If you practise and master these techniques and have a stock of at least the basic level 1 Chinese sauces in your pantry (see pages 30–1), you will always be able to cook delicious Chinese meals without having to rely on sourcing all the traditional ingredients. The point is not to be intimidated by unfamiliar ingredients or a lack of specific items for elements of a recipe. Moreover, feel free to try out the 'swapsies' in any case and see how close you can get to the essence of the original dish!

NOODLES

Noodles are considered to be symbols of good luck in Chinese tradition, as they represent long life. It is important to make sure noodles are cooked properly in order to maintain their structural integrity and add a textural component to your dish. Dried noodles are amazing store-cupboard ingredients because you can essentially make a whole meal with them in a matter of 10–15 minutes without much more than a bit of technique and a sauce or two.

There are many more varieties of noodles that you can explore in Asian supermarkets, so when trying any for the first time, just soak them in hot water from the kettle and prepare as explained opposite, then I suggest blanching them in a hot stock or soup for a simple lunch to understand their texture before using them in other ways.

FRESH NOODLES

Those bought from Chinese supermarkets are often coated in a little oil or flour to keep them moist and separated. Before using fresh noodles, separate the noodle strands carefully using your fingertips. They are then ready to use however you wish to cook them.

DRIED NOODLES

These are an essential part of a Chinese pantry. They can be stored easily in a cool, dry place and will last for several months. To prepare:

1

Put your noodles into a large mixing bowl, cover fully with hot water from the kettle and leave for 3–5 minutes (depending on the thickness of the noodles). Note: If you leave the noodles in the water for too long, they will become too soft and will not have the al dente bite that they should once cooked.

2

Once the noodles have been soaked and separated nicely (essentially when they have lost their packet shape), immediately drain them in a sieve, run them through cold water and drain again.

3

Cover a tray with a clean tea towel, place your noodles on top and leave them to dry for 10 minutes before use. Alternatively, to speed up the drying process, pop them in a fan-assisted oven with the fan function on but preferably without heat or on the lowest possible temperature for 5 minutes. The noodles are now ready to use in any way you like, whether boiling, adding to a soup, stir-frying or deep-frying.

TIP When looking for a good pack of dried noodles, if the noodles are packaged in 'nests', ensure you can see that the strands of noodles are indeed separate even if tightly woven. The little pockets of air indicate that they will separate easily when soaked.

LEVEL 1

EGG NOODLES

These are usually made from wheat flour, water, egg and oil. As well as acting as an extra binding agent, the egg adds a depth of flavour and colour.

RICE VERMICELLI/ SINGAPORE VERMICELLI

There are many types of vermicelli, which can be quite confusing. The most common is the thin Singapore rice vermicelli used for Singapore Noodles (see page 54), available both fresh and dried in most Western supermarkets. There are then the thicker Vietnamese or Jiangxi-style rice vermicelli, similar in shape and size to spaghetti but made out of rice flour instead. These noodles need very little soaking if bought dried and must be well dried and separated before stir-frying, otherwise they become very soggy and start to break up in the wok.

LEVEL 2

CHOP SUEY/CHOW MEIN ALKALINE NOODLES

For those who cannot eat egg, chop suey or chow mein noodles are a great alternative. These noodles are also made with wheat flour, water and oil but get their distinct yellow colour from traces of the alkaline lye water that is used to make them. Depending on thickness, if bought in their dried form, these noodles should only require 3–4 minutes' soaking in hot water from the kettle in preparation before finishing off in a stir-fry or soup.

HOR FUN RICE NOODLES

Available in all different shapes and sizes, these are essentially slightly thicker, flat versions of rice vermicelli. The thickness provides a totally different texture, and when soaked properly (usually for about 5–8 minutes) or bought fresh, they can feel almost a little slippery in texture. Hor fun noodles work well with caramelized sauces, such as black bean sauces, dark soy-based stir-fry sauces or in a pad thai.

MUNG BEAN VERMICELLI/ GLASS VERMICELLI

All types of bean vermicelli can be found in Asian supermarkets and convenience stores. They are good used in stir-fries as well as for warm and cold salads, as they have a slightly jelly-like texture and feel fresh and delicate on the palate. They can also be used as light alternatives for soup noodle dishes. Glass noodles are a little more robust than wheat-based noodles and can therefore withstand 3–5 minutes of boiling rather than just soaking in hot water from the kettle to prepare.

SWEET POTATO NOODLES

These come in different forms, sometimes as vermicelli (thin) or flattened, more like hor fun noodles (flat and wide). They also have a glassy, jelly-like texture and are quite light on the palate. Sweet potato noodles are fantastic for bulking out both cold and warm salads, and work well with the earthy texture and flavour of mushrooms or crispy tofu.

RICE

There are so many different types of rice globally, but here are some of the main ones used in Chinese cuisine. Some grains may require more or less water due to the amount of starch they contain and how well they absorb water. Whatever rice is used, it must be washed well and soaked in some cases before being cooked in order to remove any excess starch and to keep the grains separate. Usually, when cooking rice in larger quantities, you require a bit more water to ensure it reaches the whole surface area and cooks evenly. So I've provided these ratios here.

Note, I measure rice in a 240ml (8½fl oz) cup, holding 195g (7oz) of rice.

JASMINE RICE

Jasmine rice tends to be used to make the fluffy steamed rice that you often find in Chinese restaurants. It can be used for both steaming and frying, but when making fried rice, I would suggest using roughly 10 per cent less water than normal.

SUGGESTED RATIOS

For small quantities
(i.e. < 2 cups)
1 : 1 water-to-rice

For large quantities
(i.e. > 2 cups of rice)
1.25 : 1 water-to-rice

BASMATI RICE

This long- and skinny-grained rice is famously used in Indian cooking. It is also ideal for steaming in advance to use for fried rice, as the grains tend to keep separated better than other types of rice, such as jasmine rice.

SUGGESTED RATIOS

For small quantities
(i.e. < 2 cups)
1 : 1 water-to-rice

For large quantities
(i.e. > 2 cups of rice)
1.25 : 1 water-to-rice

AMERICAN LONG-GRAIN RICE

This rice has a distinct texture and bite to it, and is often used in Chinese takeaways as the go-to rice for fried rice. The grains of long-grain rice tend to cook more separately than the grains of jasmine rice, making it easier to stir-fry in bulk, which is great for large-scale fried-rice cooking!

SUGGESTED RATIOS

For small quantities
(i.e. < 2 cups)
1.25 : 1 water-to-rice

For large quantities
(i.e. > 2 cups of rice)
1.5 : 1 water-to-rice

STICKY RICE

As its name suggests, this rice is much stickier than the average rice grain and has a definite 'gluey' texture to it when cooked. This type of rice is used widely within southern China and Southeast Asia for both savoury and sweet dishes. It is also ground down into flours for types of dim sum pastries and desserts.

When using the rice, it is advisable to soak it for at least 2 hours before cooking to allow as much moisture to be absorbed by the grains as possible. The best way to cook the rice is to measure out the water along with the rice into a heatproof bowl or pasta bowl and then steam the rice, either in a steamer basket or in a wok (see page 111) for 30–35 minutes until sticky and cooked through.

SUGGESTED RATIOS

0.8 : 1 water-to-rice

SIMPLE BOILED/STEAMED RICE

Here's a little restaurant trick for steaming your rice for extra aroma and fragrance. If you add the optional salt and sugar seasoning, the sweet perfume of the rice is suddenly accentuated – while not an essential addition, certainly tasty!

1 cup (195g/7oz) rice
1 cup (240ml/8½fl oz) cold water
¼ teaspoon salt (optional)
½ teaspoon sugar (optional)

1
Place the rice in a saucepan with a tight-fitting lid. Put the saucepan under the tap and wash the rice well using cold running water to remove excess starch. Pour the rice and water through a sieve and wash through at least 2–3 times until the water runs more clear.

2
Drain and return the rice to the pan, pour over the measured cold water and place the pan on the hob. Cover the pan with the lid and bring the rice to the boil over a medium heat.

3
Once vigorously boiling, reduce the heat to a simmer and cook for 10 minutes.

4
Turn off the heat and leave the rice to rest for a further 10–15 minutes, keeping the lid on, to allow the rice to soak in the excess steam and fluff up well. Use a wooden spoon to fluff up the rice grains before serving.

LEVEL 1
COOKING OILS

Cooking oils form an essential part of Chinese cookery, and the cuisine's signature cooking technique, stir-frying, would be impossible to master without these high-heating oils. Their high smoking point means that you can bring your wok to a high temperature without burning the oil.

VEGETABLE OIL, CORN OIL, SUNFLOWER OIL

These three oils are commonly used in Chinese kitchens, as they all have high enough smoking points to stir-fry and deep-fry at high temperatures. They also provide an immediate seal, which is most important for these quick cooking methods.

RAPESEED OIL

Rapeseed oil has a high smoking point and is ideal for stir-frying as well as being perfect for those who are highly health conscious, as it has the lowest saturated fat content of any of the cooking oils.

GROUNDNUT OIL

Groundnut (or peanut) oil also has a very high smoking point and is therefore great for stir-frying or deep-frying. Bear in mind that you must first check if anyone you are cooking for has a peanut allergy before using.

RICE BRAN OIL

This oil is widely used in Japanese cooking and in high-end Chinese restaurants. It provides the perfect temperature for deep-frying as it has an extremely high smoking point. However, it can prove quite expensive and is consequently used less often in domestic kitchens.

LEVEL 1
SAUCES

To get a better idea of how to use each of these sauces, it's imperative to understand what each sauce lends to your cooking from a taste and texture perspective. Once you are more aware of the taste each sauce provides, it becomes easier to balance overall flavours using the different sauces, which in turn will help you to build confidence when experimenting with your own recipes. Ideally across a Chinese meal, the sauces you mix should touch different parts of your palate in a balanced way, touching on: sweet, sour, salty, savoury, spicy and bitter flavours.

The 'sacred soybean' has an obvious significance in Chinese cuisine, with fermented soybeans being used in many of the sauces that stock up our pantry.

HOISIN SAUCE

Popularized by duck and pancakes, hoisin sauce has a great texture that comes mainly from toasted fermented soybeans and sesame paste as well as a generous amount of sugar, balanced with a bit of salt. The texture and sweetness of hoisin is great for balancing sour flavours in sauces and giving a stickier finish to sauces and marinades.

CHILLI BEAN SAUCE

Chilli and fermented soybeans and broad beans are the main components of chilli bean sauce (*toban jiang*), which will lend a dish an unmistakable depth of heat, saltiness and savoury flavour. Best to work in teaspoons at a time with this sauce, as the saltiness can overpower a dish.

OYSTER SAUCE

Made from a high concentration of oyster extract, oyster sauce should be used sparingly (1–2 tablespoons at a time) to add deep savoury flavour to stir-fries, marinades and stews. Mushroom or vegetarian stir-fry sauces are great vegan alternatives to oyster sauce.

SESAME OIL

Although not a sauce per se, sesame oil gives a dish that classic 'Chinese food' smell and is most often used either at the start of the dish in a marinade or to finish it off with a toasted, nutty flavour, but rarely for frying, as it has a very low smoking point. Therefore, it goes hand in hand with the rest of the sauces in this part of the Chinese pantry. There are, however, one or two anomalies where sesame oil is used for frying at a lower heat – the Singaporean Chicken in Ginger & Garlic Paste on page 137 is a good example.

LIGHT SOY SAUCE

This sauce is the starting point of Chinese cooking and should be regarded as the Chinese equivalent of salt. Its saltiness is perfect for seasoning and marinades.

DARK SOY SAUCE

Similar to light soy sauce, dark soy sauce has added caramel, which gives it a thicker, more syrupy texture that is great for bringing colour and depth to a dish.

RICE VINEGAR

This will lend a dish much-needed sourness with a subtle savoury note, which works perfectly for balancing out stir-fry sauces with a hint of tartness or for playing the prominent role in most sweet-and-sour dishes.

LEVEL 1

DRIED & PRESERVED FOODS & SPICES

Along with certain spices, dried and preserved foods play a leading role in creating the unique flavours of Chinese cuisine. Understanding some of these key ingredients is a great place to begin your Chinese cooking adventure.

CHINESE FIVE SPICE

This spice blend can contain more than five spices, depending on who has made it, but the main ingredients are star anise, cinnamon, clove and fennel seeds. The fifth ingredient can be anything from Sichuan pepper through to mandarin peel, ginger or garlic powder, or even all of those (making 'five spice' a bit of a misnomer). These individual spices are all very strong in flavour, so use it sparingly!

WATER CHESTNUTS

These bring a great crunch to dumpling fillings, stir-fries and stews.

DRIED RED CHILLIES

These would have found their way over to China from Central and South America. They add a great punch to oils and act as a great base flavour in many stir-fries and stews.

CRISPY FRIED ONIONS

Mainly used either as a garnish or a key ingredient in rubs or savoury crumbs, or sometimes cooked into curries and stews, these not only add crunch to a dish but also a sweet/savoury flavour.

SESAME SEEDS

A unique ingredient used to add texture to a dish without overpowering other flavours, bringing a light nuttiness to your dishes.

CHILLI POWDER

While western China may be most famous for its use of chillies, a wide variety of chilli powders are used throughout China to strengthen sauces and give depth of heat to all types of dishes.

CORNFLOUR

This is the main type of flour or starch used in Chinese kitchens to thicken sauces, tenderize meats or make crispy batters (not to be confused with Latin American cornflour made from ground maize). It can easily be replaced with potato starch.

DRIED SHIITAKE MUSHROOMS

These meaty mushrooms add texture and bite. As they are dehydrated, they act like a sponge and absorb any sauces or flavour when soaked.

BAMBOO SHOOTS

In the West, bamboo shoots most often appear in canned form. To get rid of the slightly metallic taste, it's best to blanch them in hot water for 5–10 minutes, or try to find fresh or vacuum-packed bamboo shoots instead. Their unique, earthy taste and light bite are a great addition to dumpling fillings, stir-fries, curries and stews.

LEVEL 2
SAUCES

You will come across so many sauces in an Asian supermarket, all providing different textures and flavours. Here are some of my favourites; not essentials but items to add to your pantry once you have the basics to hand and are ready for your next adventures in Chinese cooking at home.

SHAO XING RICE WINE

With a taste like a savoury dry sherry or brandy, this is often used in stir-fries to add an aromatic flavour and in marinades to tenderize meats. Much like adding a few tablespoons of stock to a dish, the subtle sweetness of rice wine provides a lighter touch to what could otherwise be quite strong and overpowering stir-fry sauces.

PLUM SAUCE

Often confused with hoisin sauce, plum sauce is more like a thick, sweetened version of sweet chilli sauce and is made from fermented plums. It's the perfect accompaniment to roasted duck.

YELLOW BEAN PASTE

This is a great substitute for hoisin for those not keen on sweetness but wanting a similar texture.

SESAME PASTE

This is the epitome of savoury. With a thick, peanut butter-like texture, you have to mix it well with stock or another thin liquid to incorporate it into salad dressings, or add to sauces for a lovely consistency.

RED RICE VINEGAR

Much like black vinegar but with a more subtle, less caramelized flavour, red rice vinegar is often used for dumpling dipping sauces or to add colour and acid when basting or marinating roast meats.

SWEET CHILLI SAUCE

Sweet chilli's jam-like texture is perfect for thickening sauces without cornflour, and it has a great balance of sweet, spicy and sour.

KECAP MANIS

This highly caramelized Malaysian sweet soy sauce is great for creating sticky sauces to coat and cling to other foods. Its treacle-like flavour and texture work perfectly with naturally sour ingredients, such as tamarind.

SRIRACHA CHILLI SAUCE

A Thai-style hot chilli paste made with garlic, vinegar, salt and sugar. Its smooth texture makes it perfect for drizzling over fried rice, a noodle dish or even a posh hot dog!

SAMBAL SAUCE

A Malaysian-style chilli, tamarind and onion jam; fantastic served on the side of fried rice or soup noodles, and also works well in stir-fry recipes.

XO SAUCE

This relatively modern invention from Hong Kong and southern China has a base of chilli and garlic with dried shrimp and scallops, contributing a rich, savoury seafood flavour to any dish.

CHIU CHOW CHILLI OIL

This is for red-hot, oily stir-fries, but its best bit is actually the chilli jam layer under the oil, which holds all the sweet, salty, caramelized flavour of the slow-fried chilli flakes. The type of oil you could add to absolutely anything to enhance its flavour!

CHINKIANG RICE VINEGAR

Made from black fermented glutinous rice husks, this black rice vinegar has a unique depth of sweet, sour and savoury flavour.

CHILLI GARLIC SAUCE

A coarse chilli and garlic paste; great for adding to dipping sauces or as the base of a stir-fry. Also a handy 'swapsies' for fresh garlic and chilli.

LEVEL 2
DRIED & PRESERVED FOODS & SPICES

Here's the 'chef's playground' part of the Chinese pantry. There are so many types of dried and preserved foods on offer in Asian supermarkets to enrich your cooking with a variety of flavours and textures. Well worth playing around with!

Splitting Chinese five spice into its core elements and adding them whole to poaching liquids, stocks and oils will bring extra depth to your cooking, allowing you to then use a handful of spices to finish off your dishes. For example, the ribs for Northern Chinese Roast Lamb Ribs (see page 178) are poached with whole Sichuan peppercorns, then marinated in a spice rub before grilling to finish, imparting bold layers of flavour to what some may regard as a less desirable cut of meat.

RED FERMENTED TOFU

With a unique texture much like a creamy blue cheese, fermented tofu is often used to thicken and provide a silky-smooth finish to sauces.

DRIED GOLDEN LILY MUSHROOMS

One of the many types of dried mushroom that add meaty textures to a dish without the use of meat itself, after soaking they have a stringy feel to them that works well with noodles and steamed dishes.

PICKLED PAK CHOI

Brined in a similar way to pickled cabbage, the vinegary kick of pickled pak choi is good as a side to soupy noodles or added to fried rice or other stir-fries.

RED FERMENTED TOFU

PICKLED PAK CHOI

DRIED GOLDEN LILY MUSHROOMS

SALTED DUCK EGGS

SALTED DUCK EGGS

The Chinese have eaten salted duck eggs for centuries. Once steamed, the chalky texture of the yolk can be used to create unique Chinese sauces.

PICKLED TIANJIN CABBAGE

A special type of cabbage fermented and pickled in a salty garlic solution, its strong taste is used to add flavour to soups and steamed meats or in simple dishes like fried rice or boiled dumplings.

DRIED YELLOW SOYBEANS

Soybeans in their dried form are great for adding to vegetable stocks to provide a complex depth of flavour that you wouldn't otherwise get from onions, vegetables and herbs alone.

BLACK SESAME SEEDS

With a similar nuttiness to their white counterparts, these seeds lend a dish colour, texture and flavour.

SILKEN TOFU

Whether firm or soft, this tofu is very delicate with a great melt-in-the-mouth texture.

TAMARIND CONCENTRATE

A natural sour flavouring used in many Southeast Asian cuisines and adopted by emigrant Chinese as an alternative to the vinegars used in Mainland China.

EVAPORATED MILK

An unexpected addition to a Chinese pantry, evaporated milk is prized for its silky texture and is used to enrich sauces.

PANKO BREADCRUMBS

A Japanese ingredient in origin, panko breadcrumbs add a delicately crunchy texture that works well with the myriad Chinese deep-fried foods, but are also a fantastic way to bind and bulk out dumpling fillings, meatballs or vegan and vegetarian mixes, as they absorb excess moisture, which in turn helps to bind finely chopped ingredients together well.

PRESERVED FERMENTED BLACK BEANS

Providing a strong, assertive flavour to any dish, Chinese black beans are actually salted, dried soybeans rather than the black pulses used in Latin American cuisine. When soybeans are preserved and salted in this way, the salt is extremely prominent, so it's best to soak them in hot water before using.

DRIED SHREDDED CLOUD EAR FUNGUS

With its jelly-like feel but surprisingly crunchy texture once soaked, shredded cloud ear fungus is great for salads, rustic stews or stir-fries.

SALTED SOYBEANS

When yellow soybeans are preserved in a salty brine solution, they soften and are easy to mash into a paste, and they add a unique salty and savoury thickness to a stir-fry sauce. You can also buy pre-crushed Chinese salted soybean pastes that are similar to miso paste in texture and flavour.

DESICCATED COCONUT

Used in many cuisines throughout Asia, coconut's unique bite when dried is also very versatile. When toasted, it turns a beautiful golden brown and is great for garnishing dishes.

FENNEL SEEDS

These also have an aniseed flavour that works well with the other spices noted here. Perhaps more on the sweeter side, I find they complement citrus flavours and peel well too.

CUMIN SEEDS

The use of cumin seeds in Chinese cooking reflects the influence of Indian cuisine and can be found in certain parts of western and southern China.

CINNAMON STICKS

Although cinnamon is often used in Western desserts, if you bite directly into a piece of whole cinnamon, it will leave more of a hot, spicy flavour in your mouth. This quality works perfectly in five spice and can also help bring a sweetish heat to a stew or stock.

STAR ANISE

A dried star-shaped fruit from Southwest China, star anise gives dishes a strong and sweet aniseed flavour. It is a main component of Chinese five spice.

CLOVES

Also a key component of five spice, the menthol or aniseed flavour of cloves can be quite strong and its bittersweet nature can be overpowering, so use sparingly!

SICHUAN PEPPERCORNS

This citrusy flavoured husk of a berry, derived from the prickly ash bush in Northwest China, leaves a numbing feeling on the tip of the tongue. It is one of the main forms of heat in Sichuan-style cooking and is a feature of many five-spice mixes.

MANDARIN PEEL

Adding dried mandarin peel to stocks, sauces or rubs imparts a unique, complex, bittersweet flavour to dishes. It's best to leave the peel (or other citrus peel) in stocks for only a short period of time before removing it to avoid the bitterness overriding the natural sweetness of a dish, or to use it in marinades instead.

LEVEL 2
COOKING OILS

There are some secrets to Chinese restaurant cooking that I have picked up over the years and here's one of my favourites. Using flavoured oils to cook stir-fries, curries or stews can add an extra level of depth to your Chinese dishes and are one of those tricks that guests won't ever be able to figure out. These flavoured oils are made using the skins of garlic or ginger and the ends of spring onions, or dried red chillies and Sichuan peppercorns from your store-cupboard, so are a great way to cook with little waste and get the most flavour out of every ingredient you use. With all these oils, once cooled, you can keep them in a sealed jar for the recommended length of time.

GARLIC SKIN OIL

There is a risk of botulism with garlic oils made from raw garlic cloves, so making garlic oil from garlic skins is a great way to avoid that while using up every part of the garlic. Make sure the skins are peeled from fresh garlic cloves and are clean and dry. Put as many garlic skins as possible into a heavy-based wok or pan and cover with an oil with a high smoking point (any of the Level 1 oils on pages 30–31, except for sesame oil). Heat over a low heat for 20–25 minutes. You should see the garlic skins bubbling slightly but not fizzing and you will get a garlicky aroma from the skins almost immediately. Allow to cool, transfer to a jar and seal, then use within 7–10 days.

FRESH HOT POT CHILLI & GARLIC OIL

Heat 2–3 tablespoons of vegetable oil in a wok over a low-medium heat. Add 3 roughly chopped garlic cloves, a handful of roughly chopped dried red chillies and 1 teaspoon of Sichuan peppercorns, slowly stir the spices into the oil and fry for 1–2 minutes. Allow to cool, transfer to a jar and seal, then keep in the fridge to be on the safe side and use within 4–5 days. It is perfect for any type of spicy Sichuan or northern Chinese dish, added to the end of stir-fries or even for topping poached dishes and noodle soups.

GINGER & SPRING ONION OIL

It's a low and slow approach with this oil that uses leftovers too. Save any fresh ginger peelings and ends of spring onions, then give the spring onion ends a good wash under cold running water before patting them dry with kitchen paper. Put the ginger and spring onions into a heavy-based wok or pan and cover with an oil with a high smoking point, as for the Garlic Skin Oil opposite. Heat over a low heat for 30 minutes. You should see the peelings bubbling slightly but not fizzing and the spring onion ends should look shrivelled and completely dry by the end of the cooking process. Allow to cool, transfer to a jar and seal, then use within 7–10 days.

SICHUAN PEPPER CHILLI OIL

For a simple chilli oil, put a handful of dried red chillies and Sichuan peppercorns into a heavy-based wok or pan and cover with an oil with a high smoking point, as for the Garlic Skin Oil opposite. Heat over a low heat for 15 minutes. Allow to cool, transfer to a jar and seal, then use within 10–15 days.

THE WOK CLOCK

Now that we've covered how to use your cleaver and prep your ingredients, the next hurdle is understanding how to organize yourself before you start to cook.

I often get asked how Chinese takeaways manage to serve up a number of dishes so quickly. Aside from the amazingly powerful equipment they have access to in their commercial kitchens, there are also some basic organizational techniques they use that are invaluable when it comes to keeping your cooking quick as well as your kitchen clean and tidy. One specific technique, which we call the Wok Clock and have developed and use daily at the School of Wok, will help you to take that leap forward by setting up your ingredients in order of use before you start to cook. By doing this, you won't even have to look back at the recipe while in the throes of cooking, saving yourself time and energy without ever having to sacrifice the cooking of your ingredients while you re-read your recipe.

Once you have prepared all your ingredients, place them in their cooking order on a large round plate, starting at 12 o'clock and working your way clockwise around the plate. It's that simple! This organization is not exclusive to wok cooking ('Wok Clock' is just a simple term to remember); whether you are cooking a stir-fry or a slow-cooked curry, it works. Any recipe that has a Wok Clock within the method has a simple illustrated Wok Clock that demonstrates the preparation set-up required for the dish. Once you get into the habit of organizing your ingredients in this way, you will find cooking as a whole to be a much neater and more straightforward process, freeing you up to experience the joys of preparing dishes and learning new techniques rather than constantly scampering to consult your recipe books.

BALANCE IN CHINESE FOOD

Chinese food is all about achieving a balance of flavour, texture and colour – whether you are serving one plate or several plates of food. While there are certain individual dishes that can touch almost all your flavour sensations at the same time, to master the true skill of Chinese cooking, the more challenging scenario is being able to select a number of dishes that touch all or most of the basic tastes (sweet, sour, salty, savoury, spicy and bitter), a good combination of textures (crispy, crunchy, silky and melt-in-the-mouth, a gentle bite, or juicy and succulent) and are in turn meaty and rich or light and fresh.

If your meal covers all of the above, you are almost there! The last part of the puzzle is making sure that there is a good balance of colours (bright, dark and neutral), which is what really plays a big part in the presentation of Chinese food. Remember, we also eat with our eyes! Once you understand this balance of flavour, texture and colour, you are definitely moving towards becoming a seasoned Chinese cook.

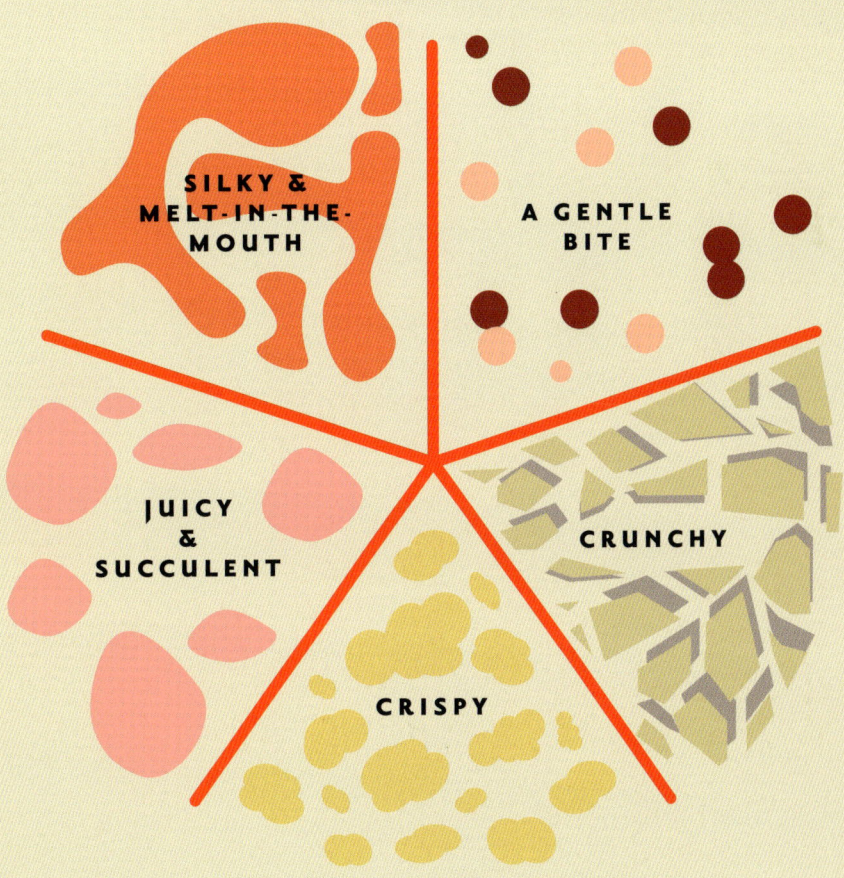

CHAPTER 1
STIR-FRYING

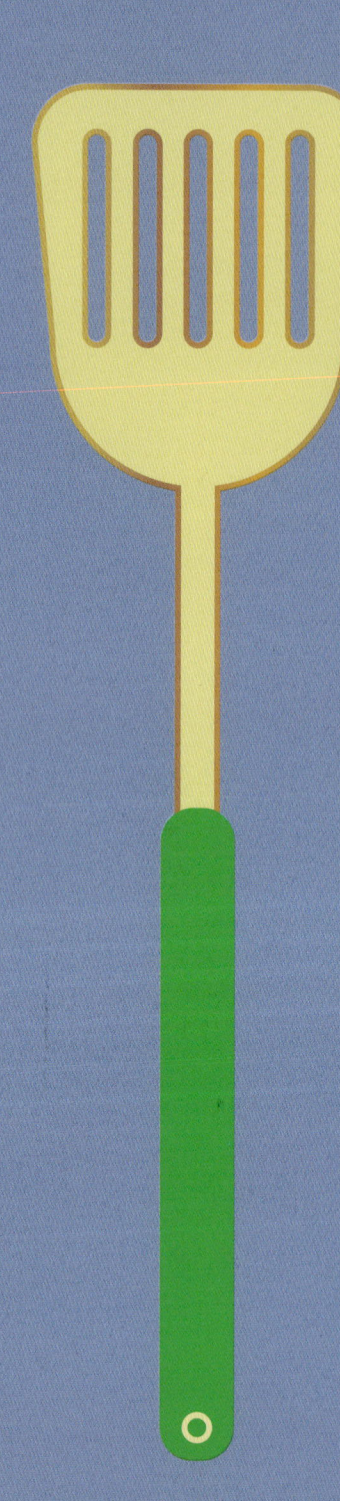

STIR-FRYING

STIR-FRYING, as its name suggests, is the technique of frying while continuously stirring or circulating heat, and it is the heat that's all-important. Stir-frying is all about *wok hei*, or 'wok's air' in English, which you can think of as the 'height of fire', or the level of heat. It's said that Chinese cooks have good *wok hei* if they have a true understanding of the heat of their wok and how to handle it in all situations, and a stir-fry's success is based on the quality of the cook's *wok hei*, as I have explained on page 49. However, although *wok hei* is dependent on a cook's natural ability to understand heat, I believe it can be learned and achieved over time by following the simple set of rules I've laid out here.

A stir-fry is, in its nature, incredibly quick to cook – your average chicken stir-fry should only take about five minutes. This is why you slice or dice your ingredients into small pieces, as it speeds up the cooking process and allows the 'height of fire' to do a quick but precise job of cooking and sealing your food.

Many Chinese chefs insist that the golden rule of wok cooking is to have an extremely hot wok and a high source of heat, and I agree. Cooking over a high heat seals the flavour into your ingredients and locks in the moisture. However, domestic kitchens don't have huge wok burners or even necessarily gas stoves, and it takes an extremely brave (or slightly crazy) home chef to be confident in dealing with a smoking-hot pan straight away.

So perhaps the key to mastering *wok hei* at home is not how to heat up your wok but actually how to cool it down. The methods outlined here will help you cook quickly but also safely, keeping the cooking heat high but giving you a bit more cooking time so that your stir-fry will be crisp and delicious – and most of all, not burned!

STIR-FRY

THE GOLDEN RULES

1
BE ORGANIZED

Always make sure you have all your ingredients 100 per cent prepared and organized before you start your cooking! Stir-frying is very quick and it will get very hectic if you are not organized before you start. The easiest way to organize yourself when stir-frying is to present all your ingredients – from harder vegetables, to meats, to softer vegetables – in a clockwise order around a plate so that you don't have to think or even look at the recipe once you start. This is what I refer to as the Wok Clock (see page 42 for more details).

2
USE OIL SPARINGLY

Add a maximum of 1 tablespoon of oil before cooking, and then add oil bit by bit (a ½ tablespoon at a time) as and when required. You need just enough oil to cover the base of the wok. If too much oil goes into the wok at the start, the first ingredient you add will absorb it all and your stir-fry will be greasy.

3
WAIT FOR THE SMOKE

Oil should be smoking hot before you add any ingredient to the wok. However, if your wok is still smoking once the ingredients are in the pan, it needs cooling down (see page 49).

4
NEVER LOSE YOUR SIZZLE

Your wok must always make a sizzling sound. At times you may need to cool your wok down, but one thing is certain when stir-frying: NEVER LOSE YOUR SIZZLE! No sizzling sound? Turn up the heat.

5
HARDER VEGGIES GO IN FIRST

Some ingredients take longer to cook than others, like harder vegetables and chicken, for example. Put these in the wok first to ensure they cook through.

6
MEAT TIMINGS

When stir-frying, meat is often finely sliced or diced to cook quickly. If you are looking for a quick one-wok-wonder, generally add the meat to the stir-fry between the harder vegetables (such as carrots, broccoli) and the softer vegetables (such as choi sum, beansprouts). If, however, you would like to go the more professional route, try blanching the meat first in a wok half full of hot oil or boiling hot water for 1–2 minutes. This extra step will help to seal in the meat's moisture and flavour. The presealed meat can then be reintroduced to the stir-fry at the end, before you add the sauce.

7
ONLY USE OILS WITH A HIGH SMOKING POINT

High-heating oils, such as vegetable, sunflower, corn, groundnut and rapeseed oil, smoke at roughly 190°C/375°F, which is much higher than olive or sesame oils (see pages 28–9). Wok cooking requires an extremely high heat, so make sure you only use those oils with a high smoking point to cook your stir-fries.

WOK HEI

HOW TO COOL DOWN YOUR WOK IN 4 SIMPLE WAYS

These tips will all help to cool your wok down when needed and circulate the smoke around your wok, training your *wok hei* in simple ways. They are well worth practising before embarking on perfecting your stir-frying skills at home.

1

STIRRING

Stir the ingredients well with your wok ladle or spatula. This will help the wok to cool down a little.

2

FOLDING

Using your ladle or spoon to fold ingredients in your stir-fry is a great way of cooling your wok down without getting food everywhere. Keep your spoon facing downwards and fold from the back into the stir-fry to help the cooling process.

3

THE WOK TOSS

Learn how to flick and toss your wok properly, giving it a long push forwards and a quick flick back. Practise with a loosely knotted tea towel or a small cup of uncooked rice and you will soon master it (although a dustpan and brush might be needed after the first few attempts!).

4

THE 'TUMMY AND HEAD MOVEMENT'

Give your food a good stir with a ladle or spatula while shaking your wok vigorously back and forth.

STIR-FRYING

PREP	**COOK**
15 minutes, plus standing & cooling	5 minutes

250g (9oz) boiled/steamed and cooled jasmine rice (see page 26)

2 eggs, well beaten

80g (2¾oz) petit pois

1 tablespoon light soy sauce

½ teaspoon sesame oil

vegetable oil

black pepper

1 spring onion, finely sliced into rings, to garnish

EGG-FRIED RICE

SERVES 2

In my opinion, every stir-frying lesson should start with this dish, the Chinese version of the classic omelette challenge of the French kitchen. It is a real test of your control of heat or *wok hei* (see page 49) – if the wok is not hot enough, the egg will stick to the base, while too hot and the food is bound to burn, leaving you with a mountain of speckled rice with bits of crunchy egg in between. And if you combine your ingredients in the wrong order, you will end up with a rice omelette. No pressure though, right? Still, master this and you will have picked up some key skills that will serve you well on your Chinese cookery journey.

1

Run a spoon through the cooked grains of rice to separate them as much as possible, breaking up any clumps. (This will help when you add the rice to the dish later.)

2

Build your wok clock. Start at 12 o'clock with the beaten egg, followed by the cooked rice, petit pois and finally the light soy sauce.

3

Heat 1 tablespoon of vegetable oil in a wok over a high heat until smoking hot. Pour in the beaten egg and allow to bubble, then scramble it slightly. Allow to bubble again, then repeat this process 2–3 times. Push the egg to one side of the wok to allow space for the next ingredients.

4

Drizzle a little more vegetable oil into the wok, add the rice and stir-fry for a minute or so, pressing into the rice to remove any clumps and separate the grains out further while cooking them through. Then add the peas and continue to stir-fry for 1 minute.

5

Pour the soy sauce over the rice and stir-fry for 30–60 seconds until the rice has absorbed it all and become drier. Once the grains of rice are 'jumping' around the base of your wok, the rice is ready (at School of Wok, we like to call this 'dancing rice').

6

Add the sesame oil and mix together well, then season with black pepper to taste and scatter over the spring onion to garnish.

PREP
20 minutes

COOK
15 minutes

400g (14oz) boneless, skinless chicken thighs, cut into 3cm (1¼ inch) wide strips

½ onion, cut into fine matchsticks

1 red pepper, cored, deseeded and cut into fine matchsticks

10 dried red chillies

2 teaspoons Sichuan peppercorns, crushed using a pestle and mortar

3 garlic cloves, finely chopped

1 birds' eye chilli, finely chopped

200g (7oz) cashew nuts

vegetable oil

1 spring onion, finely sliced, to garnish

MARINADE

1½ tablespoons cornflour

1 teaspoon sugar

large pinch of Chinese five spice

2 tablespoons light soy sauce

1 teaspoon sesame oil

SAUCE

3 tablespoons Shaoxing rice wine (swapsies: dry sherry)

1 tablespoon light soy sauce

2 tablespoons hoisin sauce

2 teaspoons chilli paste or chilli bean paste

SCHOOL OF WOK'S SICHUAN CHICKEN

SERVES 4

The region of Sichuan is situated on the western side of China and is therefore heavily influenced by ingredients from Tibet and northern India – the most significant of which, Sichuan peppercorns, have become increasingly popular in the West in recent years. These dried red berries, native to China, have a distinct fragrance when crushed and provide a unique numbing feeling all over the tongue, something the Chinese call *ma la*. They can be easily found in most Asian supermarkets.

1

Put the chicken into a mixing bowl, add the marinade ingredients and, using your hands, massage them into the strips until evenly coated.

Mix the sauce ingredients together in a small bowl or ramekin.

2

Build your wok clock. Start at 12 o'clock with the onion, red pepper and dried red chillies, followed by the marinated chicken, crushed Sichuan peppercorns and garlic, birds' eye chilli and sauce and finally the cashew nuts.

3

Heat 1 tablespoon of vegetable oil in a wok over a high heat until smoking hot. Add the onion, red pepper and dried red chillies and stir-fry for 1–2 minutes until the onion is lightly browned and slightly softened.

4

Reduce the heat to medium and push the ingredients to the side of the wok. Add another ½ tablespoon of vegetable oil to the centre of the wok and return to smoking point, then add the chicken and stir-fry for 3–5 minutes until golden brown on all sides.

5

Reduce the heat to medium, add the crushed Sichuan peppercorns and garlic and stir-fry for 2 minutes. Then add the birds' eye chilli and sauce and stir-fry over a medium-high heat for 2 minutes, or until the sauce has thickened and reduced and is sticking to the chicken. Add the cashew nuts and cook for a final 30–60 seconds, tossing the wok to combine all the ingredients well. Transfer to a large serving plate, scatter over the spring onion to garnish and serve.

TIP If you are a keen chilli eater and fancy something with a little more punch, then throw in a mixture of different types of chillies here – dried or fresh – whatever you can get your hands on.

PREP
20 minutes

COOK
5 minutes

100g (3½oz) dried Singapore vermicelli noodles

2 eggs, well beaten

½ onion, finely sliced

½ red pepper, cored, deseeded and finely sliced

6 large raw tiger or king prawns, peeled and deveined (see Tip, page 94)

handful of beansprouts, rinsed and well drained

vegetable oil

1 spring onion, finely sliced, to garnish

SPICE PASTE

1 birds' eye chilli, finely chopped

1 tablespoon water

1 tablespoon light soy sauce

½ teaspoon dark soy sauce

1 teaspoon sesame oil

1 teaspoon Madras curry powder

1–2 pinches of chilli powder (depending on how spicy you like it)

¼ teaspoon salt

SINGAPORE NOODLES

SERVES 2

This dish may not actually be Singaporean in origin, seemingly drawing on influences and crossovers in cuisine from various regions throughout Asia. It's actually the noodles – Singapore vermicelli – that give it its name. Singapore noodles are supposed to be dry, yet packed full of flavour. To get this right, follow the instructions closely and remember to keep your wok smoking hot at all times – NEVER, EVER lose your sizzle!

1
Soak the noodles in hot water for 3 minutes until they have separated. Drain and leave to dry on a clean tea towel for 10 minutes.

Mix the spice paste ingredients together in a small bowl or ramekin.

2
Build your wok clock. Start at 12 o'clock with the beaten egg, followed by the onion and red pepper, prawns, beansprouts, noodles and finally the spice paste.

3
Heat 1 tablespoon of vegetable oil in a wok over a high heat until smoking. Pour in the beaten egg and allow to bubble, then lightly scramble until cooked through.

4
Push the egg to one side of the wok to allow space for your vegetables and heat until smoking hot. (You can transfer the egg to a bowl if you prefer or only have a small wok with not enough space for the veg as well.) Add the onion and red pepper and stir-fry for 1 minute, then add the prawns and stir-fry for 30–60 seconds until lightly browned.

5
Add the beansprouts to the wok and stir-fry for 20–30 seconds, then add the noodles and stir-fry for 1 minute. Stir in the spice paste and continue to cook, stirring, until the ingredients are thoroughly combined and the noodles have dried out a little and are just starting to stick to the base of the wok. Transfer to a large serving bowl, scatter over the spring onion to garnish and serve.

TIP If you feel that the wok is looking a little dry between adding ingredients, push everything to one side with a spatula and add an extra ½ tablespoon of oil to the wok. Let the oil heat until smoking before adding the next ingredient. Note – you should never need more than 2 tablespoons of oil for a single stir-fry.

PREP	COOK
10 minutes	5 minutes

FLASH-FRIED CABBAGE WITH DRIED CHILLIES & SWEETENED SOY

SERVES 4

The first time I tried this dish I was up in the Sichuanese highlands, having driven for eight hours before stopping for lunch. I was in search of a cure for my serious 'Panger' (similar to the word 'hangry' – what we Pangs become when we aren't fed in time) and ordered this as a side to accompany a few other chilli broths, though its simple, bold flavours were so good we could easily have had it on its own. Sweet, sour, spicy and crunchy, this really is irresistibly tasty.

5–10 large dried red chillies

3 garlic cloves, finely sliced

1 medium ripe tomato, cut into eighths

1 sweetheart cabbage, cut into large chunks

vegetable or garlic oil

SAUCE

2 tablespoons Shaoxing rice wine (swapsies: dry sherry)

1 tablespoon Chinkiang vinegar (swapsies: rice vinegar)

1 tablespoon light soy sauce

¼ teaspoon dark soy sauce

½ tablespoon sugar

½ teaspoon salt

1

Mix the sauce ingredients together in a small bowl or ramekin.

2

Build your wok clock. Start at 12 o'clock with the dried red chillies and garlic, followed by the tomato and cabbage and finally the sauce.

3

Heat 1 tablespoon of vegetable or garlic oil in a wok over a high heat until smoking hot. Add the dried red chillies and garlic and stir-fry for 30 seconds. Then add the tomato and cabbage and stir-fry for 1 minute, keeping the heat high.

4

Pour the sauce into the wok, bring to a vigorous boil and stir-fry for 2–3 minutes until the cabbage is tender but still crunchy and the sauce has reduced by a third, then serve.

TIP Beware when cooking this dish, as the hot oil and chillies will create a lot of smoke! If you want to avoid the smokiness, you can add the chillies later in the cooking process, but the oil will not absorb the essence of the chillies in the same way.

PRAWN, EDAMAME & PINE NUT LETTUCE WRAPS

SERVES 2–4 AS PART OF A MEAL

PREP 20 minutes
COOK 5 minutes

This is the type of dish that I used to get as an after-school treat when we were kids, but only if my dad was home from work before my mum. Before even entering the kitchen, the aroma coming from the smoking-hot wok would hit us, and I would imagine the cheeky smirk of pride on my dad's face. He was cooking us all a 'secret snack'. This dish works as a treat that always hits the spot or even as a healthy dinner.

1 iceberg lettuce
300g (10½oz) raw prawns, peeled
½ red pepper, cored, deseeded and finely diced
150g (5½oz) edamame beans, fresh or frozen
2 garlic cloves, chopped
3 tablespoons pine nuts
vegetable oil
1 spring onion, finely sliced, to garnish

SAUCE

1 tablespoon light soy sauce
dash of sesame oil

DRESSING

6 tablespoons hoisin sauce
3 tablespoons water

1
Remove the central stalk of the lettuce by chopping off the bottom third, being careful not to tear any leaves. Turn the trimmed lettuce upside down, place it in the centre of a mixing bowl and pour over hot water very briefly, then submerge it in ice-cold water for at least a minute. (This process will help you separate the leaves from one another without much effort.) Separate and drain the individual leaves, trimming them for presentation if needed, and place in the fridge to cool.

2
To butterfly the prawns, run the blade of a sharp knife from just below the head of the prawn down the middle of the back to the tip of the tail, remove the dark vein and open up the prawn fully.

3
Mix the sauce and dressing ingredients together separately in 2 small bowls or ramekins.

4
Build your wok clock. Start at 12 o'clock with the butterflied prawns, followed by the red pepper, edamame beans and garlic, pine nuts and finally the sauce.

5
Heat 1 tablespoon of vegetable oil in a wok over a high heat until smoking hot. Add the prawns and stir-fry for 30 seconds, then add the red pepper, edamame beans and garlic and stir-fry for 1 minute, keeping the heat high.

6
Add the pine nuts and stir-fry for 30 seconds, then pour over the sauce and continue to stir-fry until the prawns are lightly browned. Transfer to a serving plate or bowl and sprinkle over the spring onion to garnish.

7
Pile the lettuce leaves on a separate plate and serve with the dressing on the side. Let everyone help themselves by filling a lettuce leaf with a spoonful of the prawn mixture, wrapping it into a bundle and dipping it into the dressing.

PREP
15 minutes

COOK
5 minutes

500g (1lb 2oz) fresh clams

2 garlic cloves, finely chopped

1 thumb-sized piece of ginger, peeled and finely chopped

2 red chillies, finely chopped

vegetable oil

small handful of coriander sprigs

SAUCE

4 tablespoons Shaoxing rice wine (swapsies: dry sherry)

4 tablespoons water

1 tablespoon light soy sauce

1 teaspoon chilli bean sauce (*toban jiang*)

½ teaspoon dark soy sauce

CHILLI & GARLIC 'WEALTHY' CLAMS

SERVES 2–4 WITH SIDE DISHES

When thinking of Hong Kong, most people picture a big, busy, skyscraper-filled city, but I immediately imagine (and can even almost taste) a giant bowl of chilli and garlic clams, enjoyed while sitting next to the seafront of Sai Kung harbour. Dotted with fishing boats, Sai Kung is nothing but low-rise houses, beaches and restaurants full of fresh seafood – quite the contrast to modern Hong Kong. The Chinese like to think that clams look like old gold bullions, and therefore represent good wealth, which is why this dish is widely eaten during Chinese New Year.

1

Sort through the clams, discarding any that don't close when tapped gently. Wash the clams thoroughly by running them under cold water and rinsing them 3 or 4 times, then put them into a large mixing bowl. Mix the sauce ingredients together in a small bowl or ramekin.

2

Build your wok clock. Start at 12 o'clock with the garlic, ginger and red chillies, followed by the clams and finally the sauce.

3

Heat 1 tablespoon of vegetable oil in a wok over a medium heat. Add the garlic, ginger and red chillies and stir-fry for 20–30 seconds until fragrant.

4

Increase the heat to high and add the clams to the wok, then immediately pour over the sauce and bring to a vigorous boil. Cover the wok with a lid and cook for 3–5 minutes, shaking occasionally, until the clams have opened up. Discard any clams that remain closed after cooking. Transfer to a large serving bowl, stir in the coriander sprigs and serve.

TIP As with all seafood, the most important issue here is not to overcook the clams – remember to control the heat of your wok by shaking it when needed in order to cook them just through but no more.

PREP
15 minutes

COOK
5 minutes

8 king scallops, cleaned

1 teaspoon cornflour

1 small knob of ginger, peeled and finely sliced

2 garlic cloves, finely sliced

bunch of large asparagus, trimmed and diagonally sliced into 2.5cm (1 inch) pieces

vegetable oil

1 spring onion, finely sliced, to garnish

SAUCE

2 tablespoons Shaoxing rice wine (swapsies: dry sherry)

1 tablespoon light soy sauce

1 tablespoon oyster sauce

1 teaspoon sesame oil

SCALLOPS & ASPARAGUS IN SHAOXING RICE WINE

SERVES 2

This light and simple recipe will show you just how easy it is to showcase the freshness of good local produce. It is best cooked in the springtime during the short asparagus season, when the vegetable is as sweet as it can be and we are starting to think about lighter, fresher flavours.

1

Put the scallops into a small mixing bowl, add the cornflour and, using your hands, gently massage it into the scallops until evenly coated.

Mix the sauce ingredients together in a separate small bowl or ramekin.

2

Build your wok clock. Start at 12 o'clock with the ginger and garlic, followed by the asparagus, scallops and finally the sauce.

3

Heat 1 tablespoon of vegetable oil in a wok over a high heat until smoking hot. Add the ginger and garlic and stir-fry for 30 seconds until slightly softened. Then add the asparagus and stir-fry for 2 minutes until just tender and lightly coloured. Transfer the ingredients to a bowl.

4

Add another 1 tablespoon of vegetable oil to the wok and heat to smoking point. Add the scallops and stir-fry for 1 minute until browned on all sides.

5

Return the vegetable mixture to the wok, then pour over the sauce, bring to a vigorous boil and cook for 30 seconds until silky smooth and just beginning to coat the scallops. Transfer to a large serving dish, scatter over the spring onion to garnish and serve.

TIP If you want more of a midweek option but something just as tasty, use raw peeled and deveined tiger or king prawns or fresh, firm tofu pieces instead of the scallops.

PREP 20 minutes **COOK** 5 minutes

SALMON BITES IN XO ONION SAUCE

SERVES 4

If you are looking for a way to spice up that weekly salmon fillet that sits in your freezer begging not to be pan-fried or baked again, then this should give you some inspiration! The sugarsnaps provide a great crunch to the dish, while the XO sauce – a type of chilli and garlic oil packed full of dried shrimp and scallops – adds a real depth of flavour to this luxurious yet simple midweek meal.

- 1 onion, finely sliced
- 3 garlic cloves, finely sliced
- 2 large red chillies, finely sliced
- 300g (10½oz) sugarsnaps
- 500g (1lb 2oz) skinless salmon fillet, pin-boned (ask the fishmonger to do this for you) and cut into 1–2cm (½–¾ inch) bite-sized pieces
- vegetable oil

SAUCE

- 200ml (7fl oz) chicken or fish stock
- 4 tablespoons XO sauce
- 2 tablespoons light soy sauce
- 2 tablespoons sweet chilli sauce
- 1 tablespoon oyster sauce
- steamed rice, to serve

1
Mix the sauce ingredients together in a jug or bowl.

2
Build your wok clock. Start at 12 o'clock with the onion, garlic and red chillies, followed by the sugarsnaps, salmon and finally the sauce.

3
Heat 1 tablespoon of vegetable oil in a wok over a high heat until smoking hot. Add the onion, garlic and chillies and stir-fry for 30 seconds until the onion is lightly browned. Then add the sugarsnaps and stir-fry for 1 minute until slightly coloured. Transfer the ingredients to a bowl.

4
Add another 1 tablespoon of vegetable oil to the wok, heat to smoking point and allow to smoke for 5 seconds to ensure the wok is hot enough for the fish to sear well without sticking. Add the salmon and stir-fry for 1–2 minutes until browned on all sides (see Tip).

5
Return the vegetable mixture to the wok, pour over the sauce and bring to a vigorous boil. Cook for 1 minute until the sauce has thickened and reduced enough to just coat the ingredients. Transfer to a large serving dish and serve with steamed rice.

TIP The best way to turn the salmon (or any fragile ingredient) in the wok while stir-frying without breaking up the delicate pieces is to use a fish slice, lifting up and folding the ingredients gently from underneath.

PAK CHOI WITH CHINESE MUSHROOM SAUCE

SERVES 2

This classic Cantonese combination works either as a lovely accompaniment to any meal or as a substantial main course with a side of rice. The meatiness and varied textures of the different mushrooms give it a great bite and a real depth of flavour. Use whatever type of fresh mushroom you can find in season, even regular button mushrooms – they all taste good!

PREP
15 minutes, plus soaking

COOK
45 minutes

- 1 thumb-sized piece of ginger, peeled and finely sliced
- 6 dried shiitake mushrooms, soaked in hot water for at least 2 hours, preferably overnight, then drained and 300ml (10fl oz) of the soaking water reserved
- 150g (5½oz) fresh wild mushrooms (such as chanterelle, cep, girolle and oyster), trimmed and cut into chunks
- 300g (10½oz) pak choi, quartered lengthways
- 2 tablespoons water
- 1 teaspoon sesame oil
- vegetable oil
- pinch of salt
- handful of roughly chopped coriander, to garnish

SAUCE

- 2 tablespoons Shaoxing rice wine (swapsies: dry sherry)
- 1½ tablespoons vegetarian oyster sauce or oyster sauce
- 1 tablespoon light soy sauce
- ½ teaspoon dark soy sauce
- ½ teaspoon sugar

1

Mix the sauce ingredients together in a small bowl or ramekin.

2

Build your wok clock. Start at 12 o'clock with the soaked dried shiitake mushrooms and half the ginger, followed by the sauce, mushroom soaking water, fresh mushrooms, the remaining ginger, pak choi, and finally the sesame oil.

3

Heat 1 tablespoon of vegetable oil in a heavy-based saucepan or clay pot over a medium heat. Add half the ginger and the soaked dried shiitake mushrooms and stir-fry for 2–3 minutes until the ginger has softened and is fragrant. Pour over the sauce and bring to a vigorous boil, then add the mushroom soaking water, return to a simmer and cook for 40 minutes, or until the sauce has reduced by half.

4

Five minutes before the mushroom sauce is ready, heat a wok over a medium-high heat, add the fresh mushrooms and flash-fry for 1 minute until lightly browned on the edges. Transfer to the sauce and leave to simmer.

5

Return the wok to the heat, add another ½ tablespoon of vegetable oil and heat until smoking hot. Add the remaining ginger and stir-fry for 20 seconds, then add the pak choi and stir-fry for 1 minute. Add the measured water, season the pak choi with a pinch of salt and drizzle over the sesame oil, then cover the wok with a lid. Cook for another 1–2 minutes until the pak choi leaves are wilted but the stalks still have their vibrant green colour.

6

Arrange the pak choi in layers on a large serving plate, then pour over the mushroom sauce garnish with the coriander and serve.

PREP
20 minutes,
plus soaking

COOK
5 minutes

100g (3½oz) dried egg noodles or chop suey-style noodles

1 carrot, cut into matchsticks

150g (5½oz) pak choi, finely sliced (swapsies: green cabbage, kale or large spinach leaves)

2 dried shiitake mushrooms, soaked in hot water for at least 2 hours, preferably overnight, then drained and finely sliced

100g (3½oz) beansprouts, rinsed and well drained

1½ tablespoons dark soy sauce

1 spring onion, cut into fine matchsticks

1 teaspoon sesame oil

vegetable or garlic oil

HONG KONG-STYLE FRIED NOODLES

SERVES 2

Noodles are a key ingredient in Chinese cookery, and learning how to handle them properly in the wok is essential. The 'tummy and head movement' (see page 49) needed to evenly distribute the vegetables among the noodles and keep each strand separate without any clumping or breaking is one that many people find difficult to grasp at first, so don't lose hope if it takes time to master. The Hong Kong tradition is to have these for breakfast alongside rice porridge and savoury doughnuts.

1

Soak the noodles in hot water for 3–5 minutes until they have separated. Drain and leave to dry on a clean tea towel for 10 minutes.

2

Build your wok clock. Start at 12 o'clock with the carrot, pak choi and soaked dried shiitake mushrooms, followed by the beansprouts, noodles, dark soy sauce, spring onion and finally the sesame oil.

3

Heat 1 tablespoon of vegetable or garlic oil in a wok over a high heat until smoking hot. Add the carrot, pak choi and soaked dried shiitake mushrooms and stir-fry for 1 minute.

4

Push the vegetables to the back of the wok, add the beansprouts and stir-fry for 20–30 seconds. Transfer all the vegetables to a large mixing bowl.

5

Heat another ½ tablespoon of vegetable oil in the wok to a high heat, add the noodles and stir-fry for 1 minute. Return the vegetables to the wok along with the dark soy sauce. Stir the noodles from the centre of the pan outwards, while shaking the wok back and forth, until they are evenly coloured by the dark soy sauce (this is what we call the 'tummy and head movement' at the School).

6

Add the spring onion and sesame oil and give everything one final stir. Transfer to a large serving bowl and serve.

TIP These noodles must be made with a good-quality Chinese dark soy sauce and should take no longer than 2–3 minutes to cook – if you control the heat correctly, the sauce should caramelize well, creating a glazed finish of dark soy and sesame oil rather than leaving the noodles swimming in sauce.

PREP	COOK
30 minutes	15 minutes

400g (14oz) minced pork or beef

½ teaspoon salt

2 garlic cloves, finely chopped

½ thumb-sized piece of ginger, peeled and finely chopped

1–2 large red chillies, finely chopped

1 teaspoon preserved fermented black beans, rinsed in cold water and drained, then lightly crushed with the back of a teaspoon

300–400ml (10–14fl oz) chicken stock or water

300g (10½oz) firm silken tofu (fresh or packaged tofu), cut into 2cm (¾ inch) cubes

vegetable oil

small handful of coriander, finely chopped, to garnish

SAUCE

2 teaspoons chilli bean paste or hot chilli paste

½ teaspoon salt

¼ teaspoon sugar

¼ teaspoon dark soy sauce

CHILLI OIL

½–1 teaspoon Sichuan peppercorns, to taste

2 tablespoons chilli flakes

1–2 tablespoons vegetable oil

CORNFLOUR SLURRY

2 teaspoons cornflour

3 tablespoons water

MAPO TOFU

SERVES 4

The literal translation of this dish, 'old pocked woman tofu', may not sound particularly appetizing, but stick with it, as the result is a lovely, spicy, broth-like dish that highlights how good tofu is at absorbing flavour. Served with a bowl of rice on the side, it's the ultimate winter one-wok wonder.

1

Put the minced meat into a mixing bowl, add the salt and, using your hands, massage it into the meat until well combined.

Mix the sauce ingredients together in a small bowl or ramekin.

For the chilli oil, toast the Sichuan peppercorns in a dry wok over a medium heat for 30–60 seconds until fragrant. Grind into a powder using a pestle and mortar or spice grinder, then mix with the chilli flakes in a small heatproof bowl. Heat the vegetable oil over a high heat until smoking hot. Remove from the heat and allow to cool for 20–30 seconds, then pour over the chilli mixture.

Mix the cornflour slurry ingredients together in another small bowl until smooth.

2

Build your wok clock. Start at 12 o'clock with the seasoned minced meat, followed by the garlic and ginger, red chillies, crushed black beans, chilli oil, sauce, stock or water, tofu and finally the cornflour slurry.

3

Heat 1–2 tablespoons of vegetable oil in a wok over a medium-high heat until smoking hot. Add the minced meat and stir-fry for 1–2 minutes until browned and separated. Transfer the meat to a bowl. Add another 1–2 tablespoons of vegetable oil to the wok and heat over a medium-high heat. Add the garlic and ginger and stir-fry for 30 seconds, then add the red chillies and crushed black beans, stir-frying for 30 seconds after each addition.

4

Add the chilli oil to the wok, return the minced meat and stir-fry for 1 minute. Then add the sauce, bring to a vigorous boil and stir-fry for a minute or so.

5

Pour the stock or water into the wok and bring to the boil, then reduce the heat to low, add the tofu and simmer for 5 minutes, stirring gently to avoid breaking up the pieces. Pour in the cornflour slurry and cook, stirring, for 1 minute until slightly thickened. Transfer to a large serving bowl, scatter over the coriander to garnish and serve.

TIP For a vegetarian alternative, swap out the minced pork for dried shiitake mushrooms, soaked in hot water for at least 2 hours, preferably overnight, then drained and finely chopped.

PREP
25 minutes, plus soaking

COOK
5–10 minutes

HUNAN-STYLE SPICY BEEF

SERVES 4

I've been cooking this dish for many years and often use it to teach Western chefs about *wok hei* as the professional wok stars out there would usually sear the meat by 'pre-blanching' it in a wok full of oil, before finishing it off in a stir-fry. At home, however, it's much easier to cook the vegetables first before searing the meat, so you don't have to use excessive amounts of oil, and can cook the whole dish without having to wash the wok in between. Just follow my advice to remove the veg in between the stir-fry, as this ensures the wok is as hot as possible when searing the beef.

300g (10½oz) rump steak, cut into large flattened slices

2 teaspoons cornflour

½ thumb-sized piece of ginger, finely sliced into matchsticks

2 garlic cloves, finely sliced

2 spring onions, chopped into 3cm (1¼ inch) lengths

½ carrot, sliced into matchsticks

½ celery stick, sliced

8 dried red chillies, soaked in hot water for 10 minutes

2 tablespoons vegetable oil

MARINADE

½ teaspoons sugar

1 teaspoon ground cumin

½ tablespoon oyster sauce

1 tablespoon rice wine

1 tablespoon light soy sauce

SAUCE

½ teaspoon ground black pepper

1 teaspoon Chiu Chow chili oil

1 teaspoon chilli bean sauce (*toban jiang*)

½ tablespoon light soy sauce

1 tablespoon oyster sauce

1 tablespoon rice wine

1 tablespoon sugar

1

Put the steak slices into a mixing bowl, add the marinade ingredients and, using your hands, massage them into the meat until evenly coated. Then add the cornflour and repeat until everything is well combined.

2

Mix the sauce ingredients together in a small bowl.

3

Build your wok clock. Start at 12 o'clock with the ginger and garlic, followed by the spring onions, carrot, celery, red chillies, the marinated beef, and finally the sauce.

4

Heat half the vegetable oil in a wok over a medium-high heat and stir-fry the ginger and garlic for 30 seconds. Follow the wok clock round until you reach the soaked chillies, stir-frying for 30 seconds between each additional ingredient. Continue to stir-fry the veg for a minute or so and then remove from the wok and place in a mixing bowl or onto a plate ready for later, creating space for the meat to be cooked.

5

Now heat the remaining vegetable oil in the wok to a high heat. Once smoking hot, add the marinated beef and press down to sear for 30 seconds–1 minute to brown on one side. Turn the meat over to sear for a further 30 seconds–1 minute and then pour the stir-fried vegetables over the top. Make sure the wok is still smoking hot, count for 10 seconds, then pour the sauce around the edge of the wok, allowing it to slip into the centre and vigorously boil. Once vigorously boiling, toss the wok and fold the meat and veg together, stir-frying for a further 30 seconds–1 minute, then serve.

PREP 20 minutes **COOK** 5 minutes

BLACK BEAN BEEF IN BEER

SERVES 4

Black bean sauce is really not hard to make, but for some reason it tends to be too overpowering or gelatinous in most restaurants and takeaways. Thanks to my Aunty Eunice, I learned an incredibly handy tip that you can use in so many dishes…and even maybe in life (we were making lobster noodles at the time): 'Get it drunk first and it'll all be OK.' Here, the addition of a fine lager or light beer to the black bean sauce really lightens it up and brings out the flavours of the black beans and ginger.

3 garlic cloves, finely chopped

1 tablespoon preserved fermented black beans, rinsed in cold water and drained

pinch of salt

400g (14oz) rump steak or rib-eye steak, finely sliced

1½ tablespoons cornflour

1 onion, finely sliced

1 green or red pepper, cored, deseeded and finely sliced

1 thumb-sized piece of ginger, peeled and finely sliced

dash of sesame oil

vegetable oil

1 spring onion, finely sliced, to garnish

MARINADE

2 tablespoons light soy sauce

2 tablespoons Shaoxing rice wine (swapsies: dry sherry)

½ tablespoon sesame oil

2 teaspoons sugar

½ teaspoon Chinese five spice

SAUCE

200ml (7fl oz) lager (swapsies: chicken or vegetable stock or light, sharp lemonade or soda water)

2 tablespoons oyster sauce

¼ teaspoon dark soy sauce

1

Put the garlic into a small bowl or ramekin with the black beans and salt, then lightly crush together with the back of a teaspoon to release their flavours.

2

Put the beef into a mixing bowl, add the marinade ingredients and, using your hands, massage them into the meat slices until evenly coated. Then add the cornflour and repeat until everything is well combined.

3

Mix the sauce ingredients together in a separate small bowl or ramekin.

4

Build your wok clock. Start at 12 o'clock with the onion and green or red pepper, followed by the ginger, garlic and black bean mixture and beef, sauce and finally the sesame oil.

5

Heat 1 tablespoon of vegetable oil in a wok over a high heat until smoking hot. Add the onion and pepper, reduce the heat to medium and stir-fry for 1 minute, or until the onion has slightly softened. Transfer the vegetables to a bowl.

6

Add another 1 tablespoon of vegetable oil to the wok, heat to smoking point and allow to smoke for 5 seconds to ensure the wok is hot enough for the meat to sear well without sticking. Add the ginger, garlic and black bean mixture and beef, spread the meat out across the base of the wok in a single layer using a wooden spoon or spatula and leave to sear for 30 seconds until browned, then turn and repeat on the other side.

7

Return the vegetables to the wok, then pour over the sauce, bring to a vigorous boil and stir-fry for 2–3 minutes until thickened and slightly reduced. Stir in the sesame oil. Spoon onto a serving plate, scatter over the spring onion to garnish and serve.

PREP 15 minutes **COOK** 25 minutes

THREE TREASURE VEGETABLES

SERVES 2

I love that some Chinese dishes like this (Di San Xian) have names that give food a deeper meaning. All three vegetables are often seen as quite humble ingredients and the simple cooking process is just as modest, yet a simple combination of the earth's treasures (a potato, an aubergine and a pepper) makes the dish sound so appealing, you just have to try it, whether you like these three particular vegetables or not!

1 large Chinese aubergine (swapsies: 1 regular aubergine), sliced into evenly sized rough wedges

1–2 tablespoons cornflour

1 white potato, peeled and chopped into evenly sized rough wedges

1 onion, chopped into wedges

1 green pepper, cored, deseeded and cut into chunks

2 garlic cloves, finely sliced

100ml (3½fl oz) vegetable stock

vegetable oil, for deep-frying

SAUCE

1 tablespoon Shaoxing rice wine (swapsies: dry sherry)

1 tablespoon light soy sauce

½ tablespoon dark soy sauce

1 teaspoon sugar

steamed rice, to serve

1

Dust the aubergine pieces in the cornflour to help protect them during the cooking process.

Mix the sauce ingredients together in a small bowl.

2

Build your wok clock. Start at 12 o'clock with the potato, followed by the dusted aubergine, onion, green pepper and garlic, sauce and finally the stock.

3

Fill a wok a third of the way up with vegetable oil and heat to 160°C/325°F, or until the tip of a wooden chopstick or skewer starts to bubble (but not fizz) after 2–3 seconds in the oil. Carefully add the potato chunks to the hot oil and fry for about 8–10 minutes until crisp around the edges. Remove with a slotted spoon and drain well on a plate lined with kitchen paper.

4

Repeat this process with the aubergine but fry for just 5–6 minutes until cooked through. Carefully pour the oil in the wok into a saucepan to cool.

5

Heat the residual oil in the wok over a high heat until smoking hot. Add the onion, green pepper and garlic and stir-fry for 1–2 minutes until slightly charred and softened. Then return the deep-fried potato and aubergine to the wok and bring back to a high heat.

6

Pour over the sauce and stir-fry for 2–3 minutes until caramelized around the vegetables. Then pour in the stock a little at a time, allowing the vegetables to absorb the stock after each addition, keeping the heat high. Serve immediately with a bowl of steamed rice on the side.

PREP
15 minutes,
plus marinating

COOK
5 minutes

FLASH-FRIED VENISON & BROCCOLI WITH GINGER & SPRING ONION

SERVES 2

Although I have managed to convince my previously vegetarian wife to eat pork belly, duck, lamb and frogs' legs (all in less than a week, I might add – I'm very persuasive!), as her family are from a Hindu background, beef is something that I will never be able to share with her. So, with her in mind, I created this dish as an alternative to a stir-fried beef. Venison steaks stay tender when flash-fried in a wok, while the sourness of the tamarind and sweetness from the kecap manis give this dish a Malaysian-Chinese feel.

- 5–10 stems of Tenderstem broccoli or Chinese broccoli (*kai lan*), cut into thirds
- 200–300g (7–10½oz) venison steaks, cut into 1–2cm (½–¾ inch) chunks
- ½ tablespoon cornflour
- 1 thumb-sized piece of ginger, peeled and cut into fine matchsticks
- 2 spring onions, cut into fine matchsticks, 1 reserved to garnish
- vegetable oil
- handful of crispy fried onions, to serve (optional)

MARINADE

- 2 tablespoons Shaoxing rice wine (swapsies: dry sherry)
- 1 tablespoon light soy sauce
- 1 teaspoon sesame oil

SAUCE

- 50ml (2fl oz) chicken stock
- 2 tablespoons tamarind concentrate (see Tip)
- 1 tablespoon hoisin sauce
- 1 tablespoon kecap manis (sweet soy sauce)

1
Bring a saucepan of water to the boil, add the broccoli or *kai lan* pieces and blanch for 2 minutes. Drain and set aside.

2
Put the venison into a mixing bowl, add the marinade ingredients and, using your hands, massage them into the meat pieces until evenly coated. Then add the cornflour and repeat until everything is well combined. For the best results, cover and marinate in the fridge overnight.

3
Mix the sauce ingredients together in a small bowl or ramekin.

4
Build your wok clock. Start at 12 o'clock with the ginger and spring onion, followed by the venison, blanched broccoli or *kai lan* and finally the sauce.

5
Heat 1 tablespoon of vegetable oil in a wok over a high heat until smoking hot. Add the ginger and the spring onion and stir-fry for 1 minute until the spring onion has softened.

6
Push the ingredients to the side of the wok, add another ½ tablespoon of vegetable oil to the centre and heat to smoking point. Add the venison, cover with the ginger and spring onion and stir-fry for 1 minute. Add the broccoli or *kai lan*, then pour over the sauce, bring to a vigorous boil and cook, stirring, for 30 seconds.

7
Spoon into a serving bowl, scatter over the reserved spring onion to garnish and the crispy fried onions, if using, and serve.

TIP Tamarind lends a dish its natural sour flavour and can be found in various forms: in its pods, with its seeds in a block of paste or as a strained concentrate. If you use it a lot, I recommend you buy the paste and thin it down with water yourself at home.

SHREDDED PORK WRAPS

PREP 30 minutes
COOK 15 minutes

SERVES 4

There are so many traditional dishes in China like this one, *jiang jiang rou si*, that still surprise me as to how Chinese cooks can take something as simple as a stir-fry and elevate it through small details like perfecting their *wok hei* (see page 49) or finishing off the dish with a nonchalant flick of Shaoxing rice wine for a touch of sweet-savoury aroma. Classically, this dish is served with a specific type of soybean wrap, but I have swapped these out for some thin omelettes to make it more accessible and allow you to focus on mastering your *wok hei* rather than stressing about sourcing ingredients.

300g (10½oz) pork shoulder steak

½ tablespoon cornflour

6 eggs, well beaten and seasoned with ½ teaspoon salt and ½ teaspoon sesame oil

½ tablespoon Shaoxing rice wine (swapsies: dry sherry)

vegetable oil

MARINADE

½ thumb-sized piece of ginger, peeled and finely chopped

½ teaspoon sugar

½ tablespoon light soy sauce

½ tablespoon Shaoxing rice wine (swapsies: dry sherry)

SAUCE

100ml (3½fl oz) chicken stock

2 tablespoons sweet bean sauce (swapsies: 1 tablespoon miso paste with 1 tablespoon hoisin sauce)

1 tablespoon Shaoxing rice wine (swapsies: dry sherry)

½ tablespoon light soy sauce

½ tablespoon sugar

1 teaspoon sesame oil

TO SERVE

1 carrot, cut into matchsticks

1 celery stick, cut into matchsticks

watercress, leaves picked

1

Place the pork in the centre of a chopping board. Hold the tip of a cleaver with your crab hand (see pages 18 and 21). Rock the cleaver up and down in a fast rocking motion and run the blade up and down the piece of meat lightly, taking care not to completely cut through it. This will make lots of little cuts across the meat, opening up the surface area to allow as much of the marinade to penetrate as possible. Then give the meat a good bash with the side of your cleaver before slicing it into thin strips.

2

Put the pork into a mixing bowl, add the marinade ingredients and, using your hands, massage them into the meat strips until evenly coated. Then add the cornflour and repeat until everything is well combined.

Mix the sauce ingredients together in a jug or small bowl.

3

Build your wok clock. Start at 12 o'clock with the seasoned beaten egg, followed by the marinated pork, sauce and finally the Shaoxing rice wine.

4

For the egg wraps, use a pad of kitchen paper to rub a little vegetable oil over the base of a small nonstick frying pan, as if you are making pancakes. Bring to a medium heat, then pour a thin layer of the beaten egg into the pan and cook for about 1 minute until fully cooked. Release the egg wrap from the pan with a spatula, transfer to a serving plate and fold over twice, ready to serve. Repeat this process, making a pile of the folded egg wraps, until all the beaten egg has been used.

5

Heat 1 tablespoon of vegetable oil in a wok over a high heat until smoking hot. Add the pork and cook for 1 minute until the meat is seared and lightly browned, then turn over and sear the other side. Once the strips are well seared and start to separate, pour in the sauce, bring to a vigorous boil and stir-fry for a minute or so until it is sticking to the meat. Add the rice wine around the edge of the wok to sizzle into the stir-fry, then serve alongside the egg wraps, carrot and celery matchsticks and watercress.

SWEET-&-SOUR PORK STRIPS

PREP 30 minutes, plus soaking

COOK 10 minutes

SERVES 4

All regions of China, in fact many cuisines worldwide, have their own distinct sweet-and-sour combinations. When School of Wok started, the first dish that anyone wanted to learn was the classic Cantonese-style sweet-and-sour chicken. This dish, however, is essentially the specific sweet-and-sour flavour that Sichuan is famous for, and it has also made its mark across the world, alongside the Cantonese sweet-and-sour chicken ball, of course.

- 300g (10½oz) pork shoulder steak or loin
- ½ red onion, finely sliced
- 100g (3½oz) bamboo shoots, finely sliced
- 1 thumb-sized piece of ginger, peeled and cut into matchsticks
- 3 garlic cloves, finely chopped
- 1½ teaspoons Sichuan peppercorns, lightly crushed using a pestle and mortar
- 2 teaspoons chilli bean paste
- 60g (2¼oz) dried shredded cloud ear fungus, soaked in hot water for at least 2 hours, then drained
- 3 tablespoons pickled cabbage or pickled pak choi (swapsies: 1 gerkin), finely sliced
- vegetable oil
- 1 spring onion, finely sliced, to garnish

MARINADE

- 2 tablespoons Shaoxing rice wine (swapsies: dry sherry)
- 1½ tablespoons light soy sauce
- 1 tablespoon cornflour
- 1½ teaspoons sesame oil
- 1 teaspoon sugar

SAUCE

- 2 tablespoons chicken stock
- 1 tablespoon Chinkiang vinegar (swapsies: rice vinegar)
- 1 tablespoon hoisin sauce
- 1 tablespoon sugar
- 1–2 teaspoons Chiu Chow chilli oil
- 1 teaspoon dark soy sauce

1

Place the pork in the centre of a chopping board. Hold the tip of a cleaver with your crab hand (see pages 18 and 21). Rock the cleaver up and down in a fast rocking motion and run the blade up and down the piece of meat lightly, taking care not to completely cut through it. This will make lots of little cuts across the meat, opening up the surface area to allow as much of the marinade to penetrate as possible. Then give the meat a good bash with the side of your cleaver before slicing it into thin strips.

2

Put the pork into a mixing bowl, add the marinade ingredients and, using your hands, massage them into the meat strips until evenly coated. Mix the sauce ingredients together in a small bowl or ramekin until the sugar has fully dissolved.

3

Build your wok clock. Start at 12 o'clock with the onion and bamboo shoots, followed by the marinated pork, ginger, garlic, Sichuan peppercorns and chilli bean paste, soaked dried cloud ear fungus and pickled vegetables and finally the sauce.

4

Heat 1–2 tablespoons of vegetable oil in a wok over a high heat until smoking hot. Add the onion and bamboo shoots and stir-fry for 1 minute. Then add the pork and stir-fry for 1 minute until golden brown.

5

Add the ginger, garlic, Sichuan peppercorns and chilli bean paste and stir-fry for 30 seconds, then add the cloud ear fungus and pickled vegetables and stir-fry for 1 minute. Pour over the sauce, bring to a vigorous boil and cook, stirring, for 1–2 minutes until slightly thickened and reduced to a coating consistency. Transfer to a serving plate or bowl, scatter over the spring onion to garnish and serve.

BLACK PEPPER TOFU

PREP 10 minutes **COOK** 10 minutes

SERVES 2

Here's a quick and simple way to punch flavour into tofu for a great midweek meal. Allowing the sauce to caramelize around the tofu before finishing off the stir-fry with the addition of the vegetable stock or water is key to getting the sponge-like texture of the tofu to absorb as much of the sauce as possible, while leaving enough to mop up with some rice or noodles on the side.

- 400g (14oz) firm fresh tofu
- ½ thumb-sized piece of ginger, peeled and roughly chopped
- 1 teaspoon very finely chopped garlic
- 1 spring onion, roughly chopped
- 1 red onion, diced
- ¼ red pepper, cored, deseeded and diced
- ¼ green pepper, cored, deseeded and diced
- 150ml (5fl oz) vegetable stock
- vegetable oil

MARINADE
- 1½ tablespoons mushroom stir-fry sauce (swapsies: oyster sauce)
- 1 teaspoon black pepper
- 1 teaspoon sesame oil

SAUCE
- 2 tablespoons Shaoxing rice wine (swapsies: dry sherry)
- 1 tablespoon light soy sauce
- 1 teaspoon dark soy sauce
- ½ tablespoon mushroom stir-fry sauce
- ½ teaspoon sugar
- ¼ teaspoon black pepper

TO SERVE
- rice or noodles

1
Drain the tofu, pat dry with kitchen paper and cut into 1cm (½ inch) cubes. Put the tofu into a mixing bowl, add all the marinade ingredients and, using your hands, mix together gently, being careful not to break up the tofu.

2
Mix the sauce ingredients together in a small bowl or ramekin.

3
Build your wok clock. Start at 12 o'clock with the marinated tofu, followed by the ginger, garlic, spring onion, red onion, red and green peppers, sauce and finally the stock.

4
Heat 1–2 tablespoons of vegetable oil in a wok over a high heat until smoking hot. Carefully add the tofu pieces to the hot oil and allow the tofu to sear on one side for 1–2 minutes, then turn over with a spatula and sear on the other side until well browned. Transfer to a plate or mixing bowl.

5
Add another 1 tablespoon of vegetable oil to the wok and heat until smoking hot. Add the ginger and stir-fry for 30 seconds, then add the garlic, spring onion, red onion and peppers, stir-frying for 30 seconds after each addition.

6
Return the tofu to the wok and bring the pan back up to smoking hot, then pour in the sauce and bring to a vigorous boil. Add the stock and cook, stirring, for another 1–2 minutes, then serve with rice or noodles.

CHAPTER 2
DEEP-FRYING

DEEP-FRYING

WHILE DEEP-FRYING MAY NOT necessarily be the healthiest of cooking processes, there is something incredibly delicious about the unique texture that it creates. In Chinese cooking, deep-fried dishes have a place in the 'balancing puzzle'. Not only do they create added texture within a meal, deep-frying also seems to engage a different sense of savoury flavour on our palates, which is why I think something deep-fried is so moreish. It is important to see this chapter as that segment of a balancing act when pieced together with a whole family meal, rather than dishes that should sit alone on the dinner table every night of the week.

The Chinese tend to use deep-frying in a variety of situations. From an instant cooking process for quick starters, finger foods and pastries to creating an immediate seal for dishes that require added crispiness or crunch. Deep-fried batters can also help tasty sauces and intense flavours stick to the food, bringing several components of a dish together, such as in sweet-and-sour chicken or tofu. Within this deep-frying chapter you will come across different pastries as well as both wet and dry batters, which will form different crispy layers around your food, showcasing a variety of deep-frying techniques and outcomes.

Deep-frying is such a big part of Chinese cooking, but it definitely falls into the more adventurous side of home cooking! Here are some handy tips on how to deep-fry in the home kitchen safely as well as successfully.

DEEP-FRYING
SAFETY RULES

1

First and foremost, when deep-frying, try not to do anything else at the same time. No multitasking!

2

Use a thick, large wok or saucepan. This will ensure the heat is easier to control without the oil heating too quickly as well as prevent the hot oil from spitting over the side.

3

Never fill the pan with oil for deep-frying more than halfway up the sides of the pan.

4

Never overfill your pan with too many ingredients either. It's best to deep-fry in batches so that the food comes out crispier rather than soaking up the oil and becoming soggy.

5

If you do have to fry your ingredients in batches and are worried that your first batch will cool down by the time you have finished your last batch of frying, after the initial frying is complete, fry all the ingredients together a second time for a minute or so, or preheat your oven to 100°C/250°F/Gas Mark ½ and place the already fried batches on a wire rack or baking tray to keep warm until you are ready to finish off your dish and serve.

6

NEVER allow your oil to get so hot that it starts to smoke. If you do see it smoking, it's best to switch the heat off and allow it to cool for at least 10 minutes before starting again. Unlike when stir-frying, if you allow such a large volume of oil to smoke in a pan, the immense heat that is created within that volume of oil will soon turn into flames, which is where deep-frying can become dangerous.

7

Always have a slotted spoon or frying mesh strainer and tongs and a plate or tray lined with 2 or 3 sheets of kitchen paper at the ready to allow your fried ingredients to drain any excess oil once cooked.

8

When draining off deep-frying oil, I find the safest way to do so is to place a metal sieve on top of a large heatproof jug or saucepan and carefully pour the oil through the sieve to collect any debris. Allow to cool down to room temperature and then throw the debris away. If the oil has just been used to deep-fry meats or starchy ingredients, you may be able to reuse the frying oil once or twice. However, if you have deep-fried fish or seafood, once cooled, I would not recommend reusing the oil at all due to the strong aroma that will taint other food the next time you use it.

9

To discard used oil, make sure the oil is completely cooled and transfer to a pouring jug, then carefully pour the oil into a used wine bottle or old oil tin or container and dispose responsibly. If you deep-fry regularly, there are many oil recycling companies that can be found online these days who recycle cooking oil and turn it into biofuel.

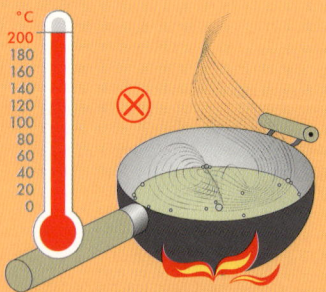

DEEP-FRYING

A STEP-BY-STEP GUIDE

Woks are perfect for deep-frying, as their large surface area allows you more room for ingredients. If using a wok to deep-fry, I would highly recommend using a flat-based wok on flat hobs so that that you are frying in the most stable and therefore safest possible way!

1

Half-fill your wok or deep-fryer with a high-heating oil – vegetable, sunflower, corn, groundnut, rapeseed or rice bran oil – and gradually heat to the desired temperature over a medium-high heat.

2

The Chinese way to test the temperature of the oil is by dipping a wooden implement – a wooden chopstick, bamboo skewer or the end of a wooden spoon – into the hot oil and resting it carefully in the liquid. At around 140°C/275°F, the wood will start to bubble slowly, but the oil will not yet be hot enough to deep-fry. At around 160–180°C/325–350°F the wood will fizz, which would suggest that you are at roughly the right temperature to deep-fry. You can of course also use a cooking probe or thermometer if you have one to hand.

3

Once the oil has reached the desired temperature, carefully place your ingredients into the hot oil using a slotted spoon or frying mesh strainer and then, once fried, remove by the same means. We tend to use a traditional bamboo mesh strainer or 'bamboo spider', where the wire mesh allows you to fish out your fried food from the oil without collecting any residual oil. Drain your deep-fried food well on a plate, tray or bowl lined with kitchen paper to soak up any excess oil.

TIP Deep-frying is essentially a sealing process – a great way of locking in the moisture and flavour of whatever you are cooking. When deep-frying correctly, your ingredients should be immersed in enough hot oil to create an immediate seal around the ingredient. As long as the heat of your oil is between 160 and 180°C/325 and 350°F, the ingredients will immediately start to blister around the edges, creating that seal that you are looking for.

SHIITAKE & CHIVE DUMPLINGS

SERVES 6 (MAKES 20–25 DUMPLINGS)

PREP 1 hour, plus soaking & drying

COOK 10 minutes

225g (8oz) plain flour, plus extra for dusting

130–150ml (4½–5fl oz) hot water

vegetable oil, for deep-frying

FILLING

50g (1¾oz) dried rice vermicelli noodles

200g (7oz) Chinese chives or garlic shoots, finely chopped

5 dried shiitake mushrooms, soaked in hot water for at least 2 hours, preferably overnight, then drained and finely chopped

5 pak choi leaves, finely chopped

1 leaf of Chinese leaf, finely chopped

1 spring onion, finely chopped

1 thumb-sized piece of ginger, peeled and finely chopped

1 garlic clove, finely chopped

handful of coriander, finely chopped

MARINADE

1 tablespoon light soy sauce

2 teaspoons sesame oil

½ tablespoon cornflour

¼ teaspoon black pepper

¼ teaspoon sugar

DIPPING SAUCE

1 thumb-sized piece of ginger, peeled and finely sliced

4 tablespoons light soy sauce

4 tablespoons Chinkiang vinegar (swapsies: rice vinegar)

There is something incredibly moreish about deep-fried dumplings with their crunchy exterior and hot, steamy filling. Like fresh pasta, dumplings should not be overcooked – whether steamed, blanched, deep- or pan-fried, the cooking process shouldn't take longer than 5 minutes. The goal is to cook the pastry and filling through, while keeping that al dente bite.

1

Sift the flour into a mixing bowl, then gradually add the measured hot water, mixing with a fork to form a dough. Knead on a lightly floured work surface for 5 minutes until slightly elastic.

2

Roll out the pastry to a thickness of 1–2mm (about 1/16th inch), then use a 7cm (2¾ inch) round pastry cutter to cut out as many pastries as possible. Set the pastries aside on a baking sheet or tray and cover with a clean tea towel until needed.

3

For the filling, soak the noodles in hot water for 3 minutes until they have separated. Drain and leave to dry on a clean tea towel for 10 minutes. Then finely chop and mix with the rest of the filling ingredients and the marinade ingredients in a mixing bowl.

4

Mix all the dipping sauce ingredients together in a small bowl or ramekin.

5

Place 1 teaspoon of the filling in the centre of each dough circle. Fold the dough over the filling to form a semicircle and pinch the top point of the semicircle tight. At each edge of the semicircle, push your finger into the point then pinch the 2 corners that have been created together, leaving 2 symmetrical Mickey Mouse ear shapes between your centre fold and the corner folds (see illustration below). Now pinch the 'ears' in towards you to make 4 layered folds. Tidy up to create a half-moon shape and place on a plate.

6

Half-fill a large pot, wok or deep-fryer with vegetable oil and heat to 180°C/350°F, or until the tip of a wooden chopstick or skewer starts to fizz after 2–3 seconds in the oil. Carefully add the dumplings to the hot oil, in batches of no more than 10, and deep-fry for 3 minutes until golden brown. Remove with a slotted spoon and drain well on a plate lined with kitchen paper. Serve the dumplings with the dipping sauce.

PREP
20 minutes, plus pickling

COOK
15 minutes

- 500g (1lb 2oz) whole sea bream, cleaned, gutted and descaled (ask the fishmonger to do this for you)
- 1 thumb-sized piece of ginger, peeled and cut into fine matchsticks
- 200g (7oz) cornflour, seasoned with ¼ teaspoon salt and ¼ teaspoon black pepper
- vegetable oil, for deep-frying

PICKLE

- ½ small red onion, finely sliced
- 4 tablespoons rice vinegar
- 1 teaspoon sugar
- ½ teaspoon salt

SAUCE

- 3 tablespoons sweet chilli sauce
- 3 tablespoons water
- 2 tablespoons rice vinegar
- 1 tablespoon light soy sauce
- dash of dark soy sauce
- 1 tablespoon sugar

CRISPY BREAM WITH PICKLED RED ONION & SWEET CHILLI DRESSING

SERVES 4

Cooking something like this at home is indeed adventurous! This is a great dish for a small dinner party – serve it with some slow-cooked meat, simple greens and rice on the side and you will have a wonderfully balanced meal. If cooked well, the skin and even bones of the fins become so crispy that you should be able to just crunch through them with your teeth. Unless it is incredibly small, deep-frying a whole fish can only be done well in a good-sized wok.

1

Put all the pickle ingredients into a small bowl and mix together well. Set aside for at least 30 minutes.

2

Make 3 diagonal cuts with a sharp knife in either side of the fish through the skin. (These cuts should be deep enough to hit the bones and will open up the flesh slightly.) Put the fish into a large bowl. Scatter the ginger inside the fish cavity and all over the fish itself. Add the seasoned cornflour and rub it into all the cracks, over the head, inside the cavity and into the slashes that you have cut until the whole fish is evenly coated.

3

Mix all the sauce ingredients together in a separate small bowl or ramekin.

4

Half-fill a large pot, wok or deep-fryer with vegetable oil and heat to 180°C/350°F, or until the tip of a wooden chopstick or skewer starts to fizz after 2–3 seconds in the oil. Carefully lay the seasoned fish in the hot oil, ensuring it is covered entirely, and deep-fry for 1–2 minutes. Reduce the heat slightly to about 160°C/325°F and continue to deep-fry for another 8–10 minutes until the fish is cooked through and golden brown all the way to its tail. Remove the fish carefully with a pair of tongs and drain well on a plate lined with kitchen paper.

5

Meanwhile, put the sauce ingredients into a saucepan or small wok and bring to a vigorous boil over a high heat.

6

Remove the sauce from the heat and pour over the cooked fish. Spoon over the pickled red onion slices and serve immediately.

TIP Cutting slits into the sides of the fish greatly speeds up the cooking process, while starting the deep-frying at a higher heat and then reducing the temperature of the oil ensures the fish will cook through without the risk of burning the outside.

PREP	COOK
1 hour	15 minutes

1 pack of spring roll pastry
1 banana, for sticking
vegetable oil, for deep-frying
sweet chilli sauce or Homemade Chilli Sauce (see page 120), to serve

FILLING

½ teaspoon salt
300g (10½ oz) duck breast
2 spring onions, finely sliced
1 red pepper, cored, deseeded and finely sliced
1 leaf of Chinese leaf, finely sliced
½ onion, finely sliced
handful of coriander, finely sliced

MARINADE

1 tablespoon oyster sauce
1 tablespoon sweet chilli sauce
2 tablespoons hoisin sauce
½ tablespoon light soy sauce
½ teaspoon dark soy sauce
1 teaspoon sesame oil

HOISIN DUCK SPRING ROLLS

SERVES 8–10

Spring roll pastries can be found in all Asian supermarkets and, surprisingly to some, in many Indian convenience stores as well, as they are used across the subcontinent for samosas and other deep-fried snacks. They have a unique elastic texture to them – this comes from the cooking process, where a thin batter is pasted onto giant heated metal rollers and slowly cooked while being rolled out at the same time. Although quite delicate, they are definitely thicker and more pliable than filo pastry.

1

Carefully separate each sheet of spring roll pastry and pile them up on a plate. Cover the pile with clingfilm to prevent the pastry from drying out.

2

For the filling, rub the salt onto the skin of the duck breast and place in a dry frying pan, skin-side down. Bring the pan to a medium-high heat and cook without any oil (plenty of fat will start to render from the duck skin) for 6 minutes, then turn and fry for 5 minutes more. Set aside to cool, then finely chop. Mix with the rest of the filling ingredients and the marinade ingredients in a mixing bowl.

3

With a pastry sheet positioned diamond-wise, follow the directions on page 86 to carefully wrap a roll. Set aside, and repeat with the rest of the pastry sheets and filling.

4

Half-fill a large pot, wok or deep-fryer with vegetable oil and heat to 180°C/350°F, or until the tip of a wooden chopstick or skewer starts to fizz after 2–3 seconds in the oil. Carefully add the spring rolls to the hot oil, in batches of no more than 10 at a time, and deep-fry for 4 minutes until golden brown. Remove with a slotted spoon and drain well on a plate lined with kitchen paper. Serve with sweet chilli sauce or the homemade chilli sauce.

WRAPPING YOUR SPRING ROLLS

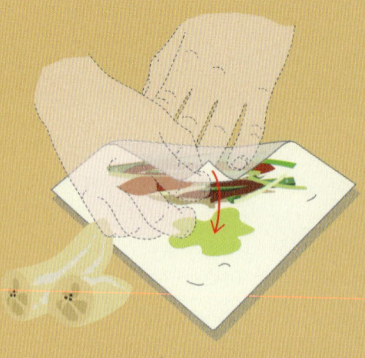

I

Cut open the banana and use it as an edible 'glue stick'. Place 1 teaspoon of the filling in the centre of the piece of pastry. Rub the banana onto the centre of the pastry, about a thumbprint above the filling.

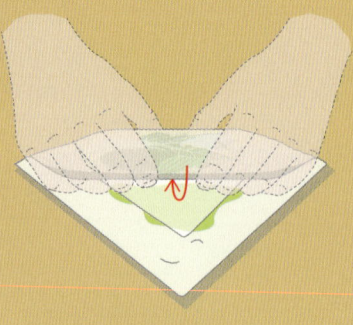

II

Fold the bottom corner up, tuck in just above the filling and stick in place with the banana, holding your fingertips over the roll and using your thumbs to roll the pastry slightly to enclose the filling.

III

Fold in the sides and stick them together with the banana.

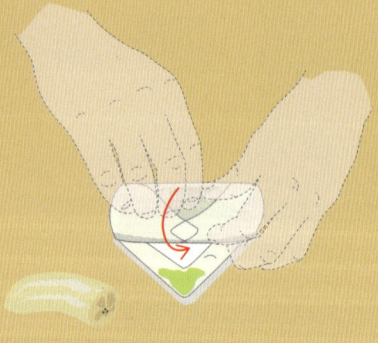

IV

Roll up the pastry and seal the seam with the banana to close.

TIP The beauty of snacks like spring rolls is that you can put pretty much whatever you like inside them. For a vegetarian spring roll, omit the duck and hoisin sauce and add beansprouts along with your favourite veg, cut into matchsticks, and use vegetarian oyster sauce in the marinade.

CRISPY CRISPY SWEET & SOUR PORK

PREP 40 minutes, plus resting
COOK 15 minutes
SERVES 2

Most people would think that sweet-and-sour pork was more of a Western Chinese invention, but the combination of a clear sweet-and-sour sauce and the unique gluey batter made traditionally out of potato starch actually comes from Dongbei in Northeast China. When deep-fried, the blobs of batter create an extra-crispy coating on the pork before being wrapped around by the syrup, which sticks to the crunchy exterior in the most satisfying way.

300g (10½oz) pork tenderloin, cut into 2–3mm (1/16–1/8 inch) thick slices
½ tablespoon bicarbonate of soda
½ thumb-sized piece of ginger, peeled and cut into matchsticks
½ carrot, cut into matchsticks
1 large red chilli, cut into matchsticks
2 spring onions, cut into matchsticks
vegetable oil, for deep-frying

MARINADE
1 tablespoon Shaoxing rice wine (swapsies: dry sherry)
½ teaspoon salt
¼ teaspoon white pepper

SAUCE
6 tablespoons rice vinegar
4 tablespoons water
4 tablespoons sugar
¼ teaspoon salt

BATTER
250g (9oz) potato starch (swapsies: cornflour)
200ml (7fl oz) water

1
Put the pork into a mixing bowl, add the bicarbonate of soda and massage into the meat pieces, then allow to rest for 10–15 minutes. Rinse the pork under cold running water to remove the excess bicarbonate of soda, drain and then squeeze it between the palms of your hands to remove any remaining moisture. Return the pork to the bowl, add the marinade ingredients and massage them into the meat pieces until evenly combined.

2
Mix the sauce ingredients together in a small bowl or ramekin until the sugar has mostly dissolved.
Mix the batter ingredients together in a mixing bowl until smooth, thick and gluey. Add the marinated pork and massage them quite vigorously into the batter so that each piece is well coated.

3
Build your wok clock. Start at 12 o'clock with the battered pork, followed by the ginger, carrot, sauce and finally the red chilli and spring onions.

4
Half-fill a wok with vegetable oil and heat to 180°C/350°F, or until the tip of a wooden chopstick or skewer starts to fizz after 2–3 seconds in the oil. Carefully add the battered pork, one piece at a time, to the hot oil and deep-fry for about 3–4 minutes until crispy (you may need to do this in 2–3 batches). Remove with a slotted spoon and drain well through a sieve set over a heatproof bowl.

5
Bring the oil back up to 180°C/350°F, then return all the pork to the oil. Fry for 1 minute. Remove and drain well on a plate lined with kitchen paper. Pour the oil in the wok through a sieve and into a saucepan to cool.

6
Heat ½ a tablespoon of vegetable oil in the wok over a high heat until smoking hot. Add the ginger and stir-fry for 30 seconds, then add the carrot and stir-fry for 30–60 seconds. Pour in the sauce, bring to a vigorous boil and slowly stir until it starts to become more syrupy and sticky. Add the crispy pork and wrap the sauce around the pieces by either tossing the wok 3–4 times or folding the pork over with your spatula. Fold in the red chilli and spring onions and then serve.

CHARRED PINEAPPLE CHICKEN IN SWEETENED BLACK RICE VINEGAR

PREP 40 minutes
COOK 30 minutes

SERVES 2

This alternative sweet-and-sour dish always brings back happy memories, as the first time I cooked it was for my very own wedding. Believe it or not, the School of Wok staff, my sisters and I prepped up enough food for 200 guests the day before the big event. If my wife wasn't tipped off beforehand that she was marrying a slightly crazy man, this certainly did the trick! The first thing we had to do to prepare this dish was dry-roast the pineapple – a process that gives it its unique flavour.

200g (7oz) fresh pineapple or drained canned pineapple

300g (10½oz) boneless, skinless chicken thighs, diagonally sliced into about 5cm (2 inch) wide pieces

200g (7oz) cornflour, seasoned with ¼ teaspoon salt and ¼ teaspoon black pepper

1 onion, cut into large chunks

1 green pepper, cored, deseeded and cut into large chunks

2 tablespoons sesame seeds, toasted in a dry wok until fragrant and golden brown

vegetable oil, for deep-frying

SAUCE

200ml (7fl oz) chicken stock

4 tablespoons Chinkiang vinegar (swapsies: rice vinegar)

2 tablespoons sugar

1 tablespoon dark soy sauce

MARINADE

1 egg, beaten

1 tablespoon light soy sauce

1 teaspoon sesame oil

½ teaspoon sugar

¼ teaspoon Chinese five spice

1

Preheat the oven to 220°C/475°F/Gas Mark 9.

Cut the pineapple into large chunks, peeling it and reserving the peelings if using fresh pineapple. Spread the pineapple chunks out onto a roasting tray and roast in the oven for 20 minutes, or until charred around the edges.

Meanwhile, put the sauce ingredients into a saucepan, adding the reserved pineapple peelings if using fresh pineapple, and bring to the boil. Reduce the heat and simmer for 15 minutes, then bring back to the boil and cook for another 5 minutes until the flavours have melded and infused and the sauce has reduced by half. Remove the pineapple peelings and pour the sauce into a small bowl.

Put the chicken into a mixing bowl, add the marinade ingredients and, using your hands, massage them into the chicken pieces until evenly coated. Then add the seasoned cornflour and massage it into the chicken. The chicken will stick together in clumps at first, but will start to separate as you continue to massage it. Once all the chicken has completely separated, it is ready to be fried.

2

Build your wok clock. Start at 12 o'clock with the coated marinated chicken, followed by the onion and green pepper, charred pineapple chunks, the reduced sauce and finally the toasted sesame seeds.

3

Half-fill a wok with vegetable oil and heat to 180°C/350°F, or until the tip of a wooden chopstick or skewer starts to fizz after 2–3 seconds in the oil. Carefully add the chicken to the hot oil and deep-fry for about 4–5 minutes until golden brown. Remove with a slotted spoon and drain well on a plate lined with kitchen paper. Carefully pour the oil in the wok through a sieve and into a saucepan to cool.

4

Heat 1 tablespoon of vegetable oil in the wok over a high heat until smoking hot. Add the onion and green pepper and stir-fry for 1 minute until nicely charred. Add the pineapple chunks, pour over the sauce and bring to a vigorous boil, then add the chicken pieces and toss through 2–3 times to mix everything together. Spoon into a serving bowl, scatter over the toasted sesame seeds and serve.

PREP
20 minutes

COOK
10 minutes

300g (10½ oz) pork shoulder steaks, cut into 2cm (¾ inch) cubes

200g (7oz) cornflour, seasoned with ¼ teaspoon salt and ¼ teaspoon black pepper

½ onion, cut into 2cm (¾ inch) dice (optional)

½ green pepper, cored, deseeded and cut into 2cm (¾ inch) dice (optional)

vegetable oil, for deep-frying

MARINADE

1 egg, beaten

1 tablespoon light soy sauce

1 teaspoon sesame oil

½ teaspoon sugar

SAUCE

4 tablespoons tomato ketchup

4 tablespoons rice vinegar or white wine vinegar

4 tablespoons sugar

½ teaspoon dark soy sauce

CLASSIC SWEET & SOUR PORK

SERVES 2

In the old days (way before the internet), sweet-and-sour was not red in colour at all, as it was predominantly made up of vinegar, sugar and dark soy sauce. However, with the heavy influence Western culture now has, the Cantonese have found that ketchup provides the perfect balance and wrapping consistency for this dish. Who's to say this recipe upgrade isn't just as authentic as the old ways? As with any culture as it changes and adapts, it doesn't make its expressions any less authentic; it just makes them a product of the times.

1

Put the pork into a mixing bowl, add the marinade ingredients and, using your hands, massage them into the meat pieces until they are evenly coated. Then add the seasoned cornflour and massage it into the meat. The meat will stick together in clumps at first, but will start to separate as you continue to massage it. Once all the meat has completely separated, it is ready to be fried. Mix the sauce ingredients together in a small bowl or ramekin.

2

Build your wok clock. Start at 12 o'clock with the coated marinated pork, followed by the onion and green pepper, if using, and finally the sauce.

3

Half-fill a wok with vegetable oil and heat to 180°C/350°F, or until the tip of a wooden chopstick or skewer starts to fizz after 2–3 seconds in the oil. Carefully add the pork to the hot oil and deep-fry for about 5–6 minutes until golden brown. Remove with a slotted spoon and drain well on a plate lined with kitchen paper. For extra crispiness, repeat the above step to double fry for a further minute. Carefully pour the oil in the wok through a sieve and into a saucepan to cool.

4

Heat 1 tablespoon of vegetable oil in the wok over a high heat until smoking hot. Add the onion and green pepper, if using, and stir-fry for 1 minute until the onion is lightly browned. Then pour over the sauce and bring to a vigorous boil. Add the pork pieces and toss through a few times to mix everything together, then serve.

TIP The key to a good sweet-and-sour is to ensure the meat is as crispy as possible and that there is just enough sauce to wrap around the meat, but not so much that the meat is swimming in it. If the sauce is not quite sticky or thick enough, continue to boil it in the wok for 30 seconds or so longer before adding the meat.

PREP
30 minutes

COOK
10 minutes

500g (1lb 2oz) baby squid, cleaned and quills removed (ask the fishmonger to do this for you), tentacles separated and bodies kept whole

200g (7oz) cornflour, seasoned with ½ teaspoon salt and ½ teaspoon pepper

vegetable oil, for deep-frying

3 garlic cloves, finely chopped

1 red chilli (or 1 birds' eye chilli if you like it hot), finely chopped

¼ teaspoon salt

½ teaspoon black pepper

2 spring onions, finely sliced, to garnish

SALT & PEPPER CHILLI SQUID

SERVES 2–4
AS PART OF A MEAL

I've been trying, testing and tweaking this recipe since my university days – endless hours of deep-frying bits of squid of all shapes and sizes in different batters. I've tried making it with egg, without egg, with different flours, in different oils, and yet I ALWAYS come back to the simplest option: no egg, just plenty of seasoned cornflour or potato starch and a vat of high-heating oil. The oil must be nice and clean to ensure you get a good golden-brown finish, which is especially important for something as waxy and delicate as squid.

1

Slice the squid bodies open to lay them flat. Run the tip of your knife along the squid pieces in a diagonal criss-cross pattern (this will help the squid curl up nicely when cooking).

2

Put the squid tubes and tentacles into a mixing bowl with the seasoned cornflour, then cover the bowl with a plate or lid, hold together firmly and shake to mix well. Using your hands, massage the cornflour into the squid until each piece is separate and as dry as possible, adding more cornflour if necessary.

3

Half-fill a wok with vegetable oil and heat to 180°C/350°F, or until the tip of a wooden chopstick or skewer starts to fizz after 2–3 seconds in the oil. Carefully add the squid pieces to the hot oil and deep-fry for 2–3 minutes until golden brown. Remove with a slotted spoon and drain well on a plate lined with kitchen paper. Carefully pour the oil in the wok through a sieve and into a saucepan to cool.

4

Heat 1 tablespoon of vegetable oil in the wok over a medium-high heat. Add the garlic, chilli, salt and black pepper, then add the squid and toss together a few times. Transfer to a serving plate, scatter over the spring onions to garnish and serve immediately.

TIP Make sure you add the squid to the wok immediately, as the chillies will kick up a lot of smoke in the pan if you hang around!

PREP
30 minutes

COOK
5 minutes

20 large raw prawns, peeled and deveined (see Tip), then finely chopped
2 garlic cloves, finely chopped
1 spring onion, finely chopped
handful of coriander, finely chopped
2 teaspoons sesame oil
1 egg white
1 tablespoon cornflour
½ stale baguette
2 teaspoons sesame seeds
vegetable oil, for deep-frying
sea salt and black pepper
sweet chilli dipping sauce, to serve

RUSTIC PRAWN TOAST

**SERVES 2–4
AS PART OF A MEAL**

While it might not be a totally authentic Chinese dish, prawn toast does embrace the Chinese culinary ethos of utilizing everything we have access to, and creating as little waste as possible. Around the corner from where my wife and I live in London there is a little French deli that sells the best fresh baguettes around (the type that go stale within 24 hours). I find these to be perfect for making a thicker, more rustic version of the classic prawn toast.

1

Put the prawns, garlic, spring onion and coriander into a mixing bowl. Season with sea salt and black pepper, add the sesame oil, egg white and cornflour and beat together with a wooden spoon.

2

Slice the baguette in half lengthways and hollow out each half of the bread, removing the soft insides. Finely dice the removed insides of the bread and add it to the prawn mixture.

3

Spoon the prawn mixture into the hollowed-out crust halves, then slice into 4cm (1½ inch) thick pieces. Sprinkle the sesame seeds over the top of each piece of bread.

4

Half-fill a large pot, wok or deep-fryer with vegetable oil and heat to 180°C/350°F, or until the tip of a wooden chopstick or skewer starts to fizz after 2–3 seconds in the oil. Carefully add the toast slices, prawn-side down (keep a slotted spoon handy to make sure they don't turn over), and deep-fry for 2–3 minutes, then turn over and fry for another 1–2 minutes until crispy and golden. Remove with a slotted spoon and drain well on a plate lined with kitchen paper. Serve immediately with sweet chilli dipping sauce on the side.

TIP To devein a prawn, run the blade of a small, sharp knife down the middle of the back to expose the dark vein, then pull it out. Alternatively, insert a cocktail stick roughly three-quarters of the way up the back of the prawn and pull the vein up and out.

PREP
20 minutes

COOK
10 minutes

300g (10½ oz) boneless, skinless chicken thighs, cut into 2–3cm (¾–1¼ inch) cubes

2 tablespoons cornflour

1 tablespoon Sichuan peppercorns

1 thumb-sized piece of ginger, peeled and cut into matchsticks

6 garlic cloves, finely sliced

20 large dried red chillies, roughly chopped

2–3 tablespoons chicken stock or water

2 tablespoons sesame seeds

vegetable oil, for frying

½ teaspoon salt

¼ teaspoon sugar

MARINADE

1 tablespoon light soy sauce

1 tablespoon Shaoxing rice wine (swapsies: dry sherry)

CHONGQING CHILLI CHICKEN

SERVES 2

In Chinese cooking, there is more to deep-frying than just submerging ingredients in hot oil to create a crispy finish. Here, the chicken is first fried in a generous amount of oil (more akin to shallow-frying) or 'blanched' in hot oil and then stir-fried with all the flavourful spices to finish. This gives the chicken a light crispy casing that cracks open in the mouth to reveal the succulent meat within. The lingering numbing sensation of the Sichuan peppercorns and crunch of the wok-fried dried chillies complements this textural heaven and elevates this artful form of deep-frying to another level.

1

Put the chicken into a mixing bowl, add the marinade ingredients and, using your hands, massage them into the chicken cubes until evenly coated. Then add the cornflour and repeat until everything is well combined.

2

Build your wok clock. Start at 12 o'clock with the coated marinated chicken, followed by the Sichuan peppercorns, ginger and garlic, dried red chillies, stock or water and finally the sesame seeds.

3

Heat 5–6 tablespoons of vegetable oil in a wok over a high heat until smoking hot. Carefully add the chicken to the hot oil, separate out the pieces with a spatula so that they are not all sticking together and fry for 2–3 minutes, folding the pieces through the oil carefully until crisp around all the edges. Set a sieve over a heatproof bowl, then carefully pour the chicken and excess oil into the sieve, reserving the hot oil.

4

Add 1 tablespoon of the reserved chicken cooking oil back to the wok and bring to a medium-high heat. Add the Sichuan peppercorns, ginger and garlic and stir-fry for 30 seconds, then add the dried red chillies and stir-fry for another 30 seconds or so.

5

Return the fried chicken to the wok and allow the heat to build for 30–60 seconds. Then pour in the stock or water and allow it to sizzle. Fold the chicken through the wok, but be careful not to toss the wok at this point, as you want the stock to penetrate the chicken.

6

Continue cooking until the liquid has evaporated, then season with the salt and sugar. Add the sesame seeds and stir-fry for about 30–60 seconds until they start to brown, then serve.

SALTED EGG PRAWNS

SERVES 2

PREP 15 minutes, plus marinating

COOK 20 minutes

Salted duck eggs are strange but wonderful ingredients. Generally preserved in either a brine solution or densely packed in charcoal, the eggs have a salted, slightly chalky feel and a very bright yolk. Because of their extreme salty taste and texture, they tend not to be eaten by themselves but rather used for making unique sauces or for serving alongside roast meats and rice or congee. In this recipe, the salted duck egg yolks are used to both thicken and flavour the wrapping sauce for the crispy prawns.

300g (10½oz) raw king prawns, peeled and deveined (see Tip, page 94)

200g (7oz) cornflour

6 fresh curry leaves

1 birds' eye chilli, finely chopped (optional)

vegetable oil, for deep-frying

MARINADE

1 egg white, beaten

½ tablespoon light soy sauce

½ tablespoon oyster sauce

1 teaspoon sugar

1 teaspoon black pepper

SAUCE

2 salted duck eggs

6 tablespoons evaporated milk

2 teaspoons sugar

pinch of salt

1

Mix the marinade ingredients together well in a mixing bowl. Add the prawns and stir until evenly coated, then cover and leave to marinate in the fridge for at least 10 minutes, preferably up to 2 hours.

2

To make the sauce, put the salted duck eggs into a heatproof dish that will fit in your wok on a steamer stand. Set the wok and steamer up (see page 111) and fill with boiling water to halfway up the sides. Place the egg dish in the wok, cover with a lid and steam for 10 minutes. Remove the eggs and allow to cool, then shell and separate the whites from the yolks. Set aside the whites for use in another recipe and crumble the yolks into a small bowl. Using the back of a spoon, blend the egg yolk into a paste, then mix with the rest of the sauce ingredients until smooth.

Add the cornflour to the marinated prawns and, using your hands, mix together until they are dry and dusty-white in colour.

3

Build your wok clock. Start at 12 o'clock with the coated marinated prawns, followed by the curry leaves and birds' eye chilli, if using, and finally the sauce.

4

Half-fill the wok with vegetable oil and heat to 180°C/350°F, or until the tip of a wooden chopstick or skewer starts to fizz after 2–3 seconds in the oil. Carefully add the prawns to the hot oil and deep-fry for about 3 minutes until golden brown. Remove with a slotted spoon and drain well on a plate lined with kitchen paper. Carefully pour the oil in the wok through a sieve and into a saucepan to cool.

5

Heat ½ a tablespoon of vegetable oil in the wok over a low heat, add the curry leaves and chilli, if using, and stir-fry for 30 seconds, until fragrant. Pour over the sauce and cook, stirring, for a minute, until slightly thickened and just starting to boil. Add the prawns and toss through to mix together, then serve immediately.

TIP Try adding the salted egg whites left over here to some Egg-fried Rice (see page 50) in place of the light soy sauce for a punchier and more fragrant result.

TEMPURA GLAZED SEA BASS

PREP 30 minutes, plus soaking

COOK 10 minutes

SERVES 2

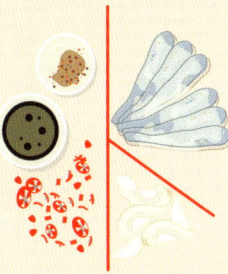

Making good tempura is not just about the batter itself, but also how to control the heat when deep-frying so that each piece of tempura is cooked evenly and crisps up well, while not sticking to another piece. It's important to get the oil to a high heat before starting to fry, and to lay each piece into the oil one by one, with at least 5–10 seconds between each other, so that you seal the battered fish one at a time. As with anything deep-fried, don't overload your oil and cook in batches if required. Once you have filled up the oil with 8–10 pieces, turn the heat down ever so slightly to cook the fish through without burning the edges of the batter.

- 1 teaspoon Sichuan peppercorns
- 2 x 100–150g (3½–5½oz) sea bass fillets, with skin, diagonally sliced into large pieces about 3cm (1¼ inches) wide
- 2 garlic cloves, finely sliced
- 5 dried red chillies, soaked in hot water for 30 minutes, then drained and roughly chopped
- vegetable oil, for deep-frying
- 1 spring onion, finely sliced into rings, to garnish

SAUCE
- 2 tablespoons sugar dissolved in 3 tablespoons hot water
- 1 tablespoon oyster sauce
- 1 tablespoon light soy sauce
- 1 teaspoon dark soy sauce

BATTER
- 100g (3½oz) plain flour
- 20g (¾oz) cornflour
- 1 egg white, beaten
- about 250ml (9fl oz) very cold soda water

1

Grind the Sichuan peppercorns to a powder using a pestle and mortar or spice grinder.

Mix the sauce ingredients together in a small bowl or ramekin.

For the batter, sift the flours together into a mixing bowl, add the egg white and mix well. Pour the cold soda water into the batter and beat well with a whisk until smooth and the consistency of single cream.

Dip the fish chunks into the batter and put them into a bowl.

2

Build your wok clock. Start at 12 o'clock with the battered fish, followed by the garlic, ground Sichuan pepper and soaked dried red chillies and finally the sauce.

3

Half-fill a wok with vegetable oil and heat to 180°C/350°F, or until the tip of a wooden chopstick or skewer starts to fizz after 2–3 seconds in the oil. Carefully lower the battered fish pieces into the hot oil and fry for 3 minutes, or until golden brown. Remove with a slotted spoon and drain well on a plate lined with kitchen paper. Carefully pour the oil in the wok through a sieve and into a saucepan to cool.

4

Heat 1 tablespoon of vegetable oil in the wok until smoking. Add the garlic and stir-fry for 20 seconds until it starts to brown. Add the ground Sichuan pepper and soaked dried red chillies, then pour over the sauce and bring to a vigorous boil. Add the fish pieces and toss through 2–3 times to mix everything together. Transfer to a serving plate, scatter over the spring onion to garnish and serve immediately.

TIP Don't keep the fish in the wok any longer than it takes to toss through 2–3 times, or it will start to lose its crispiness due to the excess heat and moisture.

PREP
45 minutes

COOK
10 minutes

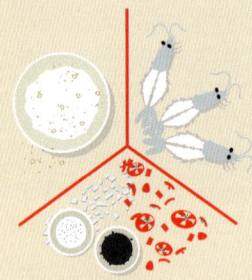

500g (1lb 2oz) shell-on, head-on raw tiger prawns

100g (3½oz) cornflour, seasoned with ¼ teaspoon salt and ¼ teaspoon black pepper

3 garlic cloves, finely chopped

1 large red chilli, finely chopped

vegetable oil, for deep-frying

¼ teaspoon salt

½ teaspoon black pepper

handful of coriander, leaves picked and stalks roughly chopped, to garnish

COCONUT SHALLOT CRUNCH

100g (3½oz) desiccated coconut

100g (3½oz) crispy fried onions

1 teaspoon salt

½ teaspoon sugar

CRISPY PRAWNS WITH COCONUT SHALLOT CRUNCH

SERVES 2

The Chinese have been in Malaysia for over ten generations now and continue to cook up and deep-fry the abundance of seafood around the country. This dish takes its influence from a type of large prawn called mantis shrimp that is very popular in Kota Kinabalu, East Malaysia, where we used to travel to as a family. Prawns or langoustines, with their sweet flesh, make a good substitute. The only hard work here is in the cleaning and picking at the prawn meat once cooked, but if you are happy to do so, it's well worth the adventure!

1

To butterfly the prawns, insert the point of a pair of kitchen scissors just below the head of the prawn and cut down the length of the shell to the tip of the tail. Then run the blade of a sharp knife down the middle of the back, remove the dark vein and open up the prawn fully.

Put the prawns into a mixing bowl with the seasoned cornflour, then cover the bowl with a plate or lid, hold together firmly and shake to mix well.

For the coconut shallot crunch, toast the desiccated coconut in a dry frying pan over a medium heat for 4–5 minutes, stirring continuously, until evenly golden brown. Allow to cool, then grind with the remaining ingredients to a fine powder using a spice or coffee grinder or pestle and mortar.

2

Build your wok clock. Start at 12 o'clock with the coated butterflied prawns, followed by the garlic, red chilli and salt and pepper, and finally the coconut shallot crunch.

3

Half-fill a wok with vegetable oil and heat to 180°C/350°F, or until the tip of a wooden chopstick or skewer starts to fizz after 2–3 seconds in the oil. Carefully add the prawns to the hot oil and deep-fry for 4–5 minutes until coral pink on the inside and golden brown on the outside. Remove with a slotted spoon and drain well on a plate covered with kitchen paper. Carefully pour the oil in the wok through a sieve and into a saucepan to cool.

4

Heat 1 tablespoon of vegetable oil in the wok over a high heat until smoking hot. Add the garlic and red chilli and season with the salt and pepper, then add the deep-fried prawns and 3 tablespoons of the coconut shallot crunch and toss together a few times.

5

Transfer to a serving plate, scatter over 1–2 tablespoons of the coconut shallot crunch and the coriander to garnish. Serve immediately.

TIP You will have more coconut shallot crunch than needed for the recipe. It is great thrown over stir-fries, grilled meat or other seafood dishes, such as the Scallops with Garlic & Vermicelli (see page 117). Cool completely, and store in an airtight container for up to 3 weeks.

PREP
20 minutes, plus marinating

COOK
10 minutes

8 chicken wings (halved or kept whole, depending on how you want to serve)
vegetable oil, for deep-frying

MARINADE

3 garlic cloves, finely sliced
1 teaspoon salt
½ teaspoon black pepper
½ teaspoon sugar
¼ teaspoon Chinese five spice

BATTER

50g (1¾oz) cornflour
1 tablespoon black sesame seeds
pinch of sea salt
pinch of black pepper
1 egg white, beaten
25ml (1fl oz) cold water

DIPPING SAUCE

1 tablespoon sriracha chilli sauce or Korean chilli paste
1 tablespoon hoisin sauce
1 tablespoon Chinkiang vinegar (swapsies: rice vinegar)
1 tablespoon sesame seeds

CHILDHOOD CHICKEN WINGS WITH STICKY CHILLI DIP

SERVES 2

No matter how much I forget as I get older, I have a steel-trap memory for food. This ability to recall selective food experiences has been passed down to me from my parents – memories in the Pang family, it seems, always hold hands with our sense of smell and taste. One of these, a plate of crispy garlic chicken wings from the 'aunty' at the poolside café by our apartment block in Singapore, has remained in the minds of both my sisters and myself since we were served it some 30-odd years ago. To this day I cannot figure out how she ever made something so simple taste just so good. Here is my best attempt.

1

Put the chicken wings into a large mixing bowl, add the marinade ingredients and, using your hands, massage them into the chicken. Cover and leave to marinate in the fridge for at least 1 hour, preferably overnight.

2

Mix the batter ingredients together in a separate mixing bowl, then add the batter to the marinated wings and mix together well until evenly coated.

3

Mix all the dipping sauce ingredients together in a small bowl or ramekin.

4

Half-fill a large pot, wok or deep-fryer with vegetable oil and heat to 160°C/325°F, or until the tip of a wooden chopstick or skewer starts to bubble (but not fizz) after 2–3 seconds in the oil. Carefully add the wings to the hot oil and deep-fry for 8–10 minutes, or until golden brown and fully cooked (see Tip). Remove with a slotted spoon and drain well on a tray lined with kitchen paper. Serve immediately along with the dipping sauce.

TIP To check if the chicken wings are fully cooked, remove one from the oil and pierce it through the middle of the thickest part with a skewer or sharp knife – the meat should be white all the way through.

SUCCULENT CRISPY CHILLI BEEF

SERVES 4

PREP	COOK
20 minutes	10 minutes

Until starting School of Wok I had actually never cooked a crispy chilli beef, as it isn't really something that I tend to associate with home-cooked Chinese food but rather a late-night takeaway.

I originally created it for one of my most loyal customers, David Jones, who was a huge advocate of the dish and, soon after learning this recipe, the School. I now have a bit of a soft spot for it, as without it, School of Wok may not have had the opportunity to become the success that it is.

200g (7oz) rump steak, cut into thin strips about 3mm (⅛ inch) wide

400g (14oz) cornflour, seasoned with ½ teaspoon salt and ½ teaspoon black pepper

1 thumb-sized piece of ginger, peeled and finely diced

3 garlic cloves, finely diced

2 birds' eye chillies, finely diced

vegetable oil, for deep-frying

large handful of coriander, finely chopped, to garnish

MARINADE

1 egg, beaten

2 tablespoons light soy sauce

2 teaspoons sesame oil

1 teaspoon sugar

SAUCE

6 tablespoons Chinkiang vinegar (swapsies: rice vinegar)

4 tablespoons honey

3 tablespoons tomato ketchup

½ tablespoon dark soy sauce

1

Put the beef into a mixing bowl, add the marinade ingredients and, using your hands, massage them into the meat pieces until they are evenly coated. Then add the seasoned cornflour and massage it into the meat. The meat will stick together in clumps at first, but will start to separate as you continue to massage it. Once all the meat has completely separated, it is ready to be fried.

Mix the sauce ingredients together in a small bowl or ramekin.

2

Build your wok clock. Start at 12 o'clock with the coated marinated beef, followed by the ginger, garlic and birds' eye chillies and finally the sauce.

3

Half-fill a wok with vegetable oil and heat to 180°C/350°F, or until the tip of a wooden chopstick or skewer starts to fizz after 2–3 seconds in the oil. Carefully add the beef to the hot oil and deep-fry for about 2–3 minutes until golden brown. Remove with a slotted spoon and drain well on a plate lined with kitchen paper. For extra crispiness, repeat the above step to double fry for a further minute. Carefully pour the oil in the wok through a sieve and into a saucepan to cool.

4

Heat ½ tablespoon of vegetable oil in the wok over a high heat until smoking hot. Add the ginger, garlic and chillies, reduce the heat to medium and stir-fry for 30 seconds until fragrant. Pour over the sauce and bring to a vigorous boil, then add the crispy beef and give the wok 2–3 tosses to mix everything together. Spoon into a serving bowl, scatter over the coriander to garnish and serve immediately.

TIP Putting the steak into the freezer 30 minutes before slicing will harden the meat and make it much easier to cut into evenly sized pieces.

CHAPTER 3
STEAMING

STEAMING

IN TRADITIONAL CHINESE culture and medicine, there is a unique term used to describe people's internal systems, food and even environments: *yeet hay*. This is a very specific and in-depth concept, with the closest possible literal translation in English being 'hot air'. It is an almost spiritual belief that our bodies are either hot or cold and that we react to different foods and cooking methods in unique ways due to our chemical balance.

Though different, you might be able to think of it much like the Ayurvedic ideas around your body type or dosha and how they affect everything you do, from your emotions to your diet. This description does not just apply to people alone. Some cooking techniques, such as deep-frying, are also considered to be *yeet hay*, although this can also change depending on the chemical balance of the person eating the cooked food. Steaming, viewed from within this cultural context, is considered to be the healthiest form of cooking in Chinese cuisine because of its delicate balance of heat and moisture and little to no oil required during the cooking process.

As with most cooking techniques, steaming is just another way of initially sealing in the flavours of what you are cooking first, then cooking them through once the heat begins to penetrate the ingredients. Due to the less intense heat of even the strongest home gas or induction hobs, steam created in a home environment (from a wok or saucepan placed on a domestic hob) is likely to act as more of an engulfing heat rather than the high-pressured steam that is created from the heavy-duty wok burners or steamers in a Chinese restaurant kitchen.

STEAMING AT HOME
A STEP-BY-STEP GUIDE

No matter which technique you are using the wok for, wok cooking shouldn't require excessive amounts of equipment – just a few key pieces will more than suffice. Steaming is no exception. While there are numerous ways of steaming in a wok, the one that I usually use (as it requires less specialist kit) is a makeshift set-up using a large, flat-based wok or a large saucepan with a stainless-steel steamer stand and domed lid (see page 111). An easy alternative is using a bamboo steamer, which sits directly on top of the wok to collect the steam. Some ingredients can stick a little to the bottom of a bamboo basket so it's usually wise to also line the basket, either with a School of Wok nonstick silicone steam mat, or with greased baking paper.

The bigger domestic bamboo steamers are usually around 26cm (10½ inches) in diameter and are great for steaming dumplings, baos, fillets of fish or anything that can fit onto a tray or plate that sits inside the steamer well. However, when steaming a whole fish or anything that needs to sit on a large plate, I usually use the improvised wok steamer set-up.

TIP The advantage that a bamboo steamer basket has over a stainless-steel steamer is that the bamboo material prevents excess water from forming on the inside of the lid and dripping onto the food (see page 16). This is very useful when steaming things like dumplings or delicate pastries, helping to keep the pastry intact.

USING A WOK, STEAMER STAND & LID

1

Place your steamer stand (or improvise with a shallow heatproof bowl) in the middle of a large, flat-based wok.

2

Fill the wok with boiling water to a third of the way up the sides.

3

Place your food for steaming on a heatproof plate so that it will sit in the wok on top of the steamer stand (or heatproof bowl). Do make sure your plate isn't so large that it doesn't allow for space between the plate and the wok's edge for you to pick it up. This will also ensure there is enough room for the steam to travel fully around the plate for proper steaming.

4

Cover the wok with a domed lid if you have one (otherwise a flatter lid will do), then steam for the required time.

USING A BAMBOO STEAMER BASKET

1

Fill your wok with boiling water a third of the way up the sides.

2

Place your food for steaming in/on a heatproof bowl or plate that will fit inside the bamboo steamer basket, or on a silicone steam mat or greased baking paper, allowing space for the lid to enclose the steam.

3

Cover the basket with the lid and place over the top of the wok, then steam for the required time.

STEAMING

AUBERGINE WITH SPRING ONION & GARLIC DRESSING

PREP 10 minutes **COOK** 15 minutes

SERVES 2

300g (10½oz) Chinese aubergines or regular aubergines
1 teaspoon salt

DRESSING

1 garlic clove, finely chopped
1 tablespoon finely chopped spring onion
1 tablespoon finely chopped coriander
1 tablespoon light soy sauce
1 tablespoon rice vinegar
1 tablespoon sugar
1 teaspoon Chiu Chow chilli oil
1 teaspoon sesame oil

Recipe testing for me is always slightly intimidating, as it is a true test of your ability to understand chemistry, flavour pairings and time management. My chef's training doesn't guarantee that the dishes will be foolproof – sometimes a bad dish just happens! Such was the case here. I had this wonderful idea of creating a complicated, slightly smoky, steamed sesame aubergine. Sadly, on the first testing it didn't work and took my wife's lovingly home-grown aubergine with it. Lesson learned: sometimes the success of a dish lies in its simplicity, as in this final version.

1

Peel the aubergines and slice them into roughly thumb-sized pieces. Put the aubergine pieces into a bowl with the salt and cover with cold water.

2

Mix the dressing ingredients together in a small bowl or ramekin until the sugar has fully dissolved.

3

Drain the aubergine pieces and lay them on a large heatproof plate that will fit in your wok on a steamer stand.

4

Set the wok and steamer up (see page 111) and fill with boiling water to halfway up the sides. Place the aubergine plate in the wok, cover with a lid and steam for 10–12 minutes, or until the aubergine is tender.

5

Remove the plate from the wok, pour the dressing over the aubergine and mix together lightly, then serve.

TIP To test whether the aubergine is cooked through, insert a fork into one of the pieces. If the fork goes straight through without any resistance, then the aubergine is ready to serve.

STUFFED TOFU WITH SOY DRESSING

PREP
30 minutes, plus soaking

COOK
15 minutes

SERVES 2

300g (10½oz) block of firm silken tofu
1–2 tablespoons cornflour
1 spring onion, sliced into rings
vegetable oil
2 tablespoons light soy sauce

STUFFING

25g (1oz) dried shiitake mushrooms, soaked for at least 2 hours, preferably overnight, in hot water, then drained, squeezed dry and finely chopped
25g (1oz) dried porcini mushrooms, soaked for at least 2 hours in hot water for 15 minutes, preferably overnight, then drained, squeezed dry and finely chopped
1 spring onion, finely chopped
1 garlic clove, finely chopped
handful of coriander, roughly chopped
2 tablespoons panko breadcrumbs
1 heaped teaspoon cornflour
1 teaspoon sesame oil
½ teaspoon sea salt
½ teaspoon black pepper

I think tofu gets a bad rap sometimes – it seems to be thought of as being almost too healthy and therefore tasteless and unappealing. For the people who say that they don't like the taste of tofu, I think it's just that they haven't had it cooked properly or in the right dish. Silken tofu works perfectly here, as it is very delicate and light in texture and when steamed develops a luxurious melt-in-the-mouth quality. I have swapped out the classic fish stuffing for the tofu itself and the combination of mushrooms flavours the tofu well while preserving its lightness and fine texture.

1

Cut the tofu block lengthways into 2cm (¾ inch) thick slices. Lay each slice flat on a plate, then cut them into 6 uniform squares. Using a teaspoon, draw a square around the inside of each slice, then scoop out half of the tofu to form a hollow, reserving the scooped-out tofu. This is where your stuffing will sit, so be careful not to cut all the way through the tofu. Spoon ¼ of a tablespoon of cornflour into each tofu hollow (this will help the stuffing to stay in place).

2

Crumble the reserved scooped-out tofu into a mixing bowl, add the stuffing ingredients and mix together well.

3

Spoon about 1–2 teaspoons of the stuffing into the hollow of each tofu slice, spreading out and flattening the mixture carefully with the back of the spoon without breaking the tofu. Using a spatula, transfer the stuffed tofu slices to a large heatproof plate that will fit in your wok on a steamer stand.

4

Set a wok up with the steamer stand and fill with boiling water to halfway up the sides. Place the stuffed tofu plate in the wok, cover with a lid and steam for 10 minutes. Remove the plate from the wok and scatter over the sliced spring onion.

5

Heat 1–2 tablespoons of vegetable oil in a small pan until smoking hot, then pour over the spring onion to create a sizzle. Spoon over the light soy sauce and serve immediately.

PREP
1 hour, plus soaking

COOK
10 minutes

300g (10½oz) minced pork

100g (3½oz) raw prawns, peeled and deveined (see Tip, page 94), then finely chopped

2 dried shiitake mushrooms, soaked in hot water for at least 2 hours, preferably overnight, then drained and finely chopped

20g (¾oz) cornflour

20 fresh wonton pastries

10 king scallops, cleaned and roes removed if buying whole, halved lengthways

kecap manis (sweet soy sauce), to serve (optional)

MARINADE

1 tablespoon sesame oil

1 teaspoon sugar

½ egg white, beaten

½ teaspoon salt

½ teaspoon black pepper

SCALLOP SIU MAI

SERVES 8-10

Although I have been eating them pretty much since I was able to eat solid food, my real dim sum journey started back in 2011 when I went to Singapore to learn how to make them from scratch. On the first day of class, my teacher made sure that I made a minimum of 500 of each type before I could move on to the next, as getting each one to look identical takes time. With these open wontons, practice makes perfect – but don't be put off! They will taste good however they end up looking and are a great addition to any dinner party.

1

Put the minced pork, prawns, soaked dried shiitake mushrooms and cornflour into a mixing bowl, add the marinade ingredients and, using your hands, mix together, then beat it – scooping it up then throwing it back into the bowl. This forms a smooth paste, tenderizes the meat and pushes any air out of the mixture.

2

Cut the wonton pastries into circles using a 6.5cm (2½ inch) pastry cutter. Place 1½ teaspoons of the filling in the centre of a pastry circle and, using the back of the teaspoon, spread the filling out over the pastry, ensuring it covers the pastry completely edge to edge.

3

Create an 'egg cup' shape with your left hand and insert the pastry so that it rests on top, with the centre drooping into the palm of your hand. With your free hand, use the base of your spoon as a 'lid' to ensure all the meat stays in the parcel, while gently turning the pastry with your left hand using the thumb and index finger and squashing the parcel sides firmly against the filling to stick. The aim is to form a uniform dumpling with slightly 'crimped' walls of pastry tightly fitting around the filling (see illustration below).

4

Once all your dumplings have been made, place half a scallop on top of each.

5

Line a bamboo steamer basket with a silicone steam mat or greased baking paper. Put the dumplings inside the basket, cover with the lid and place over a wok half-filled with boiling water. Steam for 8 minutes. Serve with kecap manis (sweet soy sauce).

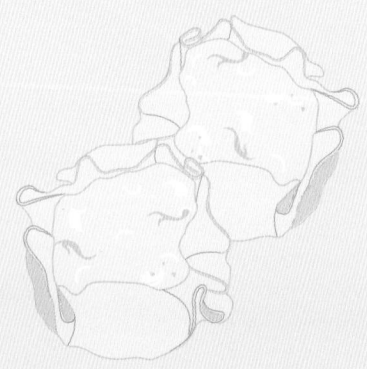

SCALLOPS WITH GARLIC & VERMICELLI

SERVES 2–3

PREP 20 minutes, plus soaking
COOK 5 minutes

100g (3½oz) nest of dried mung bean vermicelli noodles

6 scallop shells (ask the fishmonger for these)

6 king scallops, roes attached, cleaned

5 garlic cloves, finely chopped

1 spring onion, finely sliced into rings, to garnish

SAUCE

2 garlic cloves, finely chopped

1 thumb-size piece of ginger, peeled and sliced

1 spring onion, finely chopped

1 birds' eye chilli, finely chopped

handful of coriander leaves, finely chopped

2 tablespoons light soy sauce

1 tablespoon dark soy sauce

1 tablespoon hoisin sauce

2 teaspoons sugar

1 teaspoon chilli oil

1 teaspoon sesame oil

I love the way the flavour of scallops speaks for itself. Having said that, their natural sweetness can be accentuated by stronger flavours (the chilli sauce below, for example), but you don't want to add too much for fear of drowning them. This recipe is a bit like a game of Jenga, stacking as much onto one scallop shell as possible. It is a simple but much-loved, if not slightly luxurious, starter to any Chinese meal.

1
Mix the sauce ingredients together in a bowl or small ramekin until the sugar has fully dissolved.

2
Soak the noodles in hot water for 10 minutes until soft. Drain, then cut them into small pieces with scissors.

3
Arrange the scallop shells on a large heatproof plate that will fit in your wok on a steamer stand. Divide the noodles between the scallop shells, then top each with a scallop. Scatter over the garlic.

4
Set the wok and steamer up (see page 111) and fill with boiling water to halfway up the sides. Place the scallop plate in the wok, cover with a lid and steam for 3–5 minutes, depending on the size of the scallops (see Tip).

5
Remove the scallop plate from the wok. Drizzle the sauce over the scallops, scatter over the spring onion rings to garnish and serve immediately.

TIP To check whether the scallops are cooked, press a finger gently into the scallop meat: if it gives some resistance, the scallop will be cooked through properly.

PREP
15 minutes

COOK
10 minutes

24 shell-on, head-on raw river shrimps or fresh prawns

HOMEMADE CHILLI SAUCE

2 spring onions, cut into fine matchsticks

2 large red chillies, cut into fine matchsticks

1 thumb-sized piece of ginger, peeled and cut into fine matchsticks

6 tablespoons light soy sauce

6 tablespoons water

1 tablespoon dark soy sauce

1 tablespoon sugar

2 teaspoons Shaoxing rice wine (swapsies: dry sherry) – optional

RIVER SHRIMP WITH HOMEMADE CHILLI SAUCE

SERVES 4

Fresh river shrimps have a naturally sweet and savoury flavour, which means they rarely require any additional marinating or flavouring – just a little steam and a bit of chilli sauce on the side. We buy these for the School of Wok from an inconspicuous fishmonger who supplies live lobsters, crabs and fresh prawns to all the local restaurants from his store tucked away behind the main streets in London's Chinatown. If you can't get your hands on river shrimp, fresh regular prawns work well here too.

1

To devein the shrimps or prawns while keeping them intact, insert a cocktail stick roughly three-quarters of the way up the back of the shrimp or prawn and pull the dark vein up and out of the shell. Arrange the shrimps or prawns on a heatproof plate that will fit in your bamboo steamer basket.

2

Put the shrimp/prawn plate inside the basket, cover with the lid and place over a wok half-filled with boiling water. Steam for 8–10 minutes (see Tip), or until the shrimps or prawns are coral pink in colour and cooked through.

3

Meanwhile, mix all of the chilli sauce ingredients together in a small bowl.

4

Remove the plate from the steamer and serve with the chilli sauce on the side.

TIP Depending on the size of the shrimps or prawns, the steaming process may be quicker than 8 minutes. They will become quite rubbery when overcooked, so be sure to remove them from the heat as soon as they have turned coral pink in colour.

PREP
10 minutes

COOK
15 minutes

350–500g (12oz–1lb 2oz) skate wing (swapsies: salmon fillet)

1 thumb-sized piece of ginger, peeled and finely sliced

1 garlic clove, finely chopped

2 teaspoons preserved fermented black beans, rinsed in cold water and drained

pinch of salt

1 spring onion, sliced lengthways

vegetable oil

1 tablespoon light soy sauce

BLACK BEAN SKATE WING

SERVES 2

An underrated fish, most people tend to avoid skate when they walk past it in the shops, yet it couldn't be easier to deal with when cooking. From its lack of needle-like bones to its soft, flaky white meat, there just isn't anything else quite like it. You can, of course, cook this with any other type of fish fillet too.

1
Put the fish into a dish that will fit in your large wok on a steamer stand, with enough space to cover the wok or pan completely with a lid. Arrange the ginger slices on top of the fish.

2
Put the garlic into a small bowl or ramekin with the black beans and salt, then lightly crush together with the back of a teaspoon. Spoon the mixture over the fish, then spread it over evenly.

3
Set the large wok up with the steamer stand and fill with boiling water halfway up the sides. Place the fish dish in the wok or pan, cover with the lid and steam for 7–15 minutes until the flesh is falling off the fish when tested with a fork. Remove the fish from the pan and scatter over the spring onion.

4
Heat 2 tablespoons of vegetable oil in a frying pan over a high heat until smoking hot, then carefully pour the hot oil over the top of the fish. Spoon over the soy sauce and serve immediately.

TIP Try not to move the fish around too much while cooking, as the delicate flesh benefits from being barely touched. This dish is best served directly from the dish that it sits on during the steaming process.

PREP
15 minutes

COOK
15 minutes

SEA BASS WITH CRUSHED SOYBEANS & CHILLI SAUCE

SERVES 2

Much like a portrait painter, sometimes I am 'commissioned' to create a recipe that matches a dish that a student has once eaten. While it is undoubtedly a challenge to create something that lives up to expectations, when the commission is successfully fulfilled, the reward is well worth it. This recipe started out as one such commissioned dish, but over the years I have adapted it slightly, making it more about the fish itself rather than fulfilling a specific brief. It's delicious and works perfectly served with simple blanched greens on the side. Salted soybeans, found in most Chinese supermarkets, add a nice texture to the sauce, but if you can't get them, the dish works just as well without.

- 350–500g (12oz–1lb 2oz) whole sea bass, cleaned, gutted and descaled (ask the fishmonger to do this for you)
- 1 tablespoon salted soybeans, lightly crushed with the back of a teaspoon
- 2 garlic cloves, finely chopped
- 1 birds' eye chilli, finely chopped
- large handful of coriander, roughly chopped, half reserved to garnish
- vegetable oil

SAUCE

- 100ml (3½fl oz) chicken or vegetable stock, or hot water
- 1 tablespoon hoisin sauce
- 1 tablespoon Shaoxing rice wine (swapsies: dry sherry)
- 1 teaspoon chilli bean sauce (*toban jiang*)
- dash of dark soy sauce

1

Mix the sauce ingredients together in a jug or small bowl.

Place the sea bass on a large heatproof plate or platter that will fit into your large wok or steamer pan on a steamer stand.

2

Build your wok clock. Start at 12 o'clock with the sea bass, followed by the crushed salted soybeans, garlic, birds' eye chilli and sauce and finally the coriander.

3

Set the large wok up with the steamer stand and fill with boiling water halfway up the sides. Place the fish plate in the wok or pan, cover with a lid and steam for 7–12 minutes until cooked (see Tip). Remove the fish plate and set aside, covering the fish with foil so that it stays warm and moist.

4

Drain and dry the wok. Add 1 tablespoon of vegetable oil and heat until smoking hot. Add the crushed salted soybeans and stir-fry for 30 seconds, then add the garlic, chilli and sauce. Bring to a vigorous boil, then add half the coriander and continue to cook for 1 minute until the sauce has thickened and reduced by at least a third.

5

Pour the sauce over the steamed fish, garnish with the remaining coriander and serve immediately.

TIP To check whether your fish is fully cooked, pull the dorsal fin (the one on the back) lightly. If it falls off without any force, the fish will be cooked through to the bone. Remove from the pan and set aside.

PREP	COOK
20 minutes, plus soaking	30 minutes

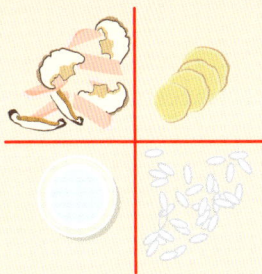

CLAY-POT CHICKEN & MUSHROOM RICE WITH CHILLI & GARLIC SAUCE

SERVES 4

Steam in cooking doesn't always have to come from water boiling in a pan. In this Hong Kong dish, the steam is created from the rice, and there is an art to getting the chicken into it at the right time in order to cook it through perfectly and give you the textures you want – a crispy layer of rice on the base of the pot, followed by fluffy, steamed rice in the middle and succulent meat on top.

400g (14oz) boneless, skinless chicken thighs, cut into 5mm (¼ inch) thick slices

8 dried shiitake mushrooms, soaked in hot water for at least 2 hours, preferably overnight, then drained and finely sliced

280g (10oz) jasmine rice

1 thumb-sized piece of ginger, peeled and finely sliced

340ml (12fl oz) water

vegetable oil

1 spring onion, finely sliced, to garnish

SAUCE

½ tablespoon vegetable oil

1 large red chilli, roughly chopped

2 garlic cloves, bashed and peeled but kept whole

6 tablespoons dark soy sauce

1 tablespoon sugar

MARINADE

2 tablespoons light soy sauce

2 tablespoons Shaoxing rice wine (swapsies: dry sherry)

1 tablespoon cornflour

2 teaspoons sesame oil

1 teaspoon sugar

1

For the sauce, heat the vegetable oil in a small saucepan over a medium heat. Add the red chilli and garlic and cook, stirring, for 30 seconds. Then add the dark soy sauce and sugar to the pan, bring to the boil and cook for 30 seconds until the sauce has caramelized slightly but is still runny. Pour into a ramekin and set aside.

Put the chicken into a mixing bowl. Add the soaked dried shiitake mushrooms and the marinade ingredients and, using your hands, massage them together until all the marinade has been absorbed.

Rinse the rice 2–3 times in cold water to get rid of any excess starch, then drain.

2

Build your wok clock. Start at 12 o'clock with the ginger, followed by the rice, measured water and finally the marinated chicken and shiitake mushroom mixture.

3

Heat 1½ tablespoons of vegetable oil in a clay pot or heavy-based saucepan to a medium heat. Add the ginger and stir-fry for 30 seconds until fragrant. Then add the rice and fry for 1 minute, stirring to coat the grains evenly in the oil. Pour over the measured water and bring to the boil, then reduce to a simmer. Add the chicken and shiitake mushroom mixture, cover the pan with a lid and cook over a low heat for 20 minutes.

4

Remove the lid and check that the chicken is cooked (it should be light brown or white in colour, with no pink), and that the rice has formed a crisp, golden brown layer on the base of the pan. If it needs it, leave it to cook for a few minutes longer. Spoon into bowls, garnish with the spring onion and serve with the sauce.

TIP If you hear light 'crackling' noises from the base of the pan during the last stage of cooking, this is a sign that the rice is crisping up. If, however, you smell burning, turn the hob off and serve immediately!

PREP
1 hour,
plus soaking

COOK
10 minutes

20 fresh wonton pastries

FILLING

150g (5½oz) raw tiger prawns, peeled and deveined (see Tip, page 94), then finely diced (optional)

3 dried shiitake mushrooms, soaked in hot water for at least 2 hours, preferably overnight, then drained and finely chopped

2 leaves of Chinese leaf, finely chopped

10–15 Chinese chives, finely chopped (swapsies: a 50:50 mixture of spring onion and chives)

large handful of coriander, finely chopped, plus extra to garnish

1 spring onion, finely chopped

1 garlic clove, finely chopped

1 tablespoon light soy sauce

2 teaspoons sesame oil

½ teaspoon sugar

BROTH

200ml (7fl oz) chicken stock

½ tablespoon oyster sauce

2 teaspoons Chiu Chow chilli oil

WONTONS IN CHILLI BROTH

SERVES 4

When it comes to learning about Chinese pastries, wontons are the best starting point. The pastry comes ready-made either fresh or frozen in most Asian supermarkets, and is very much like an egg pasta – made from egg, a medium- to high-gluten wheat flour (similar to plain flour), hot water and oil. The method of folding here creates a shape much like a gold ingot (pre-20th-century Chinese currency), and it is said that if you can fold your wontons in such a shape, you are giving your friends and family plenty of good wealth for years to come!

1
Put all the filling ingredients into a mixing bowl and mix together well.

2
With a wonton pastry positioned diamond-wise, follow the directions opposite to carefully wrap a wonton. Set aside, and repeat with the rest of the pastries and filling. Put all the wontons into a large, deep heatproof bowl that will fit into your wok on a steamer stand.

3
For the broth, bring the stock to a simmer in a saucepan, then stir in the oyster sauce and chilli oil. Pour the broth over the wontons.

4
Set the wok and steamer up (see page 111) and fill with boiling water to halfway up the sides. Put the wonton bowl into the wok, cover with a lid and steam for 6–8 minutes until the wontons have shrivelled slightly and are cooked through. Remove from the wok and serve, garnished with a little chopped coriander.

TIP These dumplings can be frozen once made before cooking. They must then be cooked from frozen, rather than allowing them to defrost and lose their shape, and must be cooked for 2 minutes longer than the specified cooking time for cooking fresh.

WRAPPING
YOUR WONTONS

I

Place 1 teaspoon of filling in the centre of each pastry. Using the tip of your finger, wet all sides of the pastry with cold water.

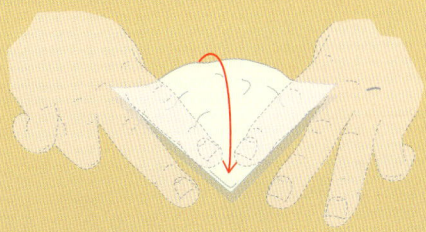

II

Fold the bottom corner over the filling to the top corner and press the pastry down to seal all sides (to form a triangle).

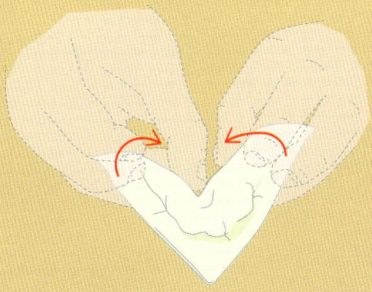

III

Holding the base of the filling with your thumbs, pull the 2 corners of the triangle towards each other, (in the school, we like to call this the 'Dark Knight Rising' as it looks roughly like a Batman shape).

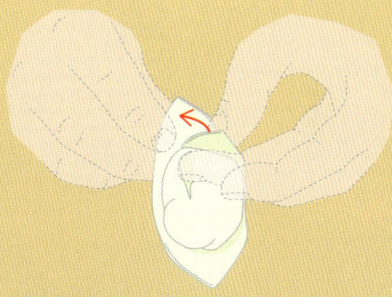

IV

Overlap the ends and press together to form a 'gold ingot/trough' shape. Set aside and fold the rest of the wontons the same way.

STEAMING

PREP
10 minutes

COOK
10 minutes

2 x 150g (5½oz) trout fillets, with skin, descaled

CHILLI BEAN, GARLIC & GINGER OIL

2 garlic cloves, finely diced

1 thumb-sized piece of ginger, peeled and finely chopped

1 spring onion, finely diced

½ tablespoon chilli bean sauce (*toban jiang*)

¼ teaspoon salt

¼ teaspoon sugar

¾ tablespoon vegetable oil

TROUT WITH CHILLI BEAN, GARLIC & GINGER OIL

SERVES 2

For me, a weekday meal needs to be healthy, quick, easy to prepare and good value for money – no one wants to use up the food budget on after-work meals rather than long, lingering weekend treats. With its vibrant colours and strong flavours, this ticks all the boxes, and is perfect for getting you out of that post-work pasta rut we all get stuck in from time to time.

1

Mix together all the ingredients for the chilli bean, garlic and ginger oil except the vegetable oil in a heatproof bowl. Heat the vegetable oil in a wok over a high heat until smoking hot, then pour over the ingredients in the bowl to create a sizzle. Stir together well and set aside.

2

Place the fish fillets on a heatproof plate that will fit into your wok on a steamer stand.

3

Set the wok and steamer up (see page 111) and fill with boiling water halfway up the sides. Place the fish plate in the wok, cover with a lid and steam for 8–10 minutes until the fish is cooked. (To test this, poke a cocktail stick into the thickest part of each fillet – if it goes through without any resistance, the fish is ready to serve.)

4

Remove the plate from the wok, spoon over the chilli bean, garlic and ginger oil to coat the fish fillets well and serve immediately.

TIP If you fancy varying this recipe, try it with salmon fillets or white fish fillets, such as sea bass or bream.

PREP
10 minutes

COOK
20 minutes

300–500g (10½–1lb 2oz) whole sea bass or bream, cleaned, gutted and descaled (ask the fishmonger to do this for you)

½ thumb-sized piece of ginger, peeled and finely sliced

2 spring onions, finely sliced into matchsticks, to garnish

vegetable oil

SAUCE

2 tablespoons light soy sauce

½ teaspoon sugar

FISH WITH GINGER & SPRING ONIONS

SERVES 2–3

In Chinese tradition, serving a whole fish at the dinner table signifies abundance in life, and if you ever see a Chinese family tucking into a whole steamed fish at a restaurant, it is most probably a special occasion of some sort. From a purely culinary perspective, one wonderful thing about this tradition is that the fish itself retains all its moisture and flavour as well as its delicate texture. In Hong Kong, the typical fish for this dish would be grouper, but sea bass and bream are also great alternatives and have a very similar flavour and texture.

1
Put the fish into a heatproof dish that will fit in your large wok on a steamer stand, with enough space to cover the wok or pan completely with a lid.

2
Arrange the ginger slices on top of the fish and inside its cavity.

3
Place the spring onions for the garnish in cold water to curl.

4
Mix the sauce ingredients together in a small bowl or ramekin until the sugar has fully dissolved.

5
Set the wok and steamer up (see page 111) and fill with boiling water halfway up the sides. Place the fish dish in the wok or pan, cover with a lid and steam for 8–15 minutes until the fish is cooked (see Tip). Remove the fish from the pan. Drain the curled spring onions and scatter them over the fish.

6
Heat 2 tablespoons of vegetable oil in a frying pan until smoking hot. Carefully pour the hot oil over the spring onions and fish to create a sizzle, then spoon over the sauce and serve immediately.

TIP When it comes to cooking whole fish, I tend to categorize them into the following sizes for cooking times: small fish (less than 300g/10½oz) 8–9 minutes; medium fish (300g–500g/10½–1lb 2oz) 10–12 minutes; and large fish (500g–750g/1lb 2oz–1lb 10z) 13–15 minutes.

FIVE SPICE LOTUS LEAF CHICKEN WITH CHINESE SAUSAGE

PREP
30 minutes, plus soaking

COOK
30 minutes

SERVES 6

Lotus leaves have a porous nature that makes them perfect for steaming – as the steam soaks through them, their sweet, earthy aroma is imparted on whatever is wrapped inside. Here they accentuate the naturally warm flavours of the five spice and wind-dried sausage, while the lotus root adds a nice contrast in texture. This is a great dinner-party dish; serve the lotus parcels whole and let the guests unwrap their individual parcels.

10 boneless, skinless chicken thighs, cut into eighths

2 wind-dried Chinese sausages, finely sliced (swapsies: any dried sausage, such as cooking chorizo)

20 dried golden lily mushrooms, soaked in hot water for at least 2 hours, preferably overnight, then drained (swapsies: finely sliced soaked dried porcini, shiitake or straw mushrooms)

6 large lotus leaves, soaked in hot water for 30–60 minutes, then drained

2 x 8–10cm (3¼–4 inch) lotus root segments (see Tip), peeled and finely sliced into rings

MARINADE

3 tablespoons light soy sauce

2 tablespoons Shaoxing rice wine (swapsies: dry sherry)

2 tablespoons cornflour

2 teaspoons sugar

2 teaspoons sesame oil

½ teaspoon Chinese five spice

TO SERVE

steamed rice

Pickled Carrot & Daikon (see page 203) or other pickled vegetable dish

1
Put the chicken, Chinese sausages and soaked dried golden lily mushrooms into a mixing bowl, add the marinade ingredients and, using your hands, massage them into the meat until everything is well combined.

2
To assemble the lotus leaf wraps, lay a leaf on a clean work surface and arrange a few of the lotus root slices in the centre. Spoon some of the marinated chicken mixture over the lotus root, then wrap the edges of the leaf around the filling to form a tight package. Repeat with the remaining leaves and chicken mixture.

3
Put the lotus leaf wraps inside a bamboo steamer basket, cover with the lid and place over a wok half-filled with boiling water. Steam for 25 minutes.

4
Remove the wraps from the steamer and serve with steamed rice and Pickled Carrot & Daikon or another pickled vegetable dish.

TIP You will find lotus root in most Chinese supermarkets; they usually come vacuum-packed. Look for the kind that is pale brown in colour – try to avoid the black-skinned lotus roots, as they tend to be older and not as fresh.

PREP
10 minutes,
plus marinating

COOK
25 minutes

15 pork ribs, chopped into 3–4cm (1¼–1½ inch) chunks (ask the butcher to do this for you)

1 large red chilli, finely sliced

1 spring onion, finely sliced, to garnish

MARINADE

2 garlic cloves, finely chopped

2 tablespoons preserved fermented black beans, rinsed in cold water and drained, then lightly crushed with the back of a teaspoon

2 tablespoons plum sauce

2 tablespoons water

1 tablespoon cornflour

2 teaspoons sugar

2 teaspoons sesame oil

1 teaspoon Chiu Chow chilli oil

1 teaspoon salt

1 teaspoon black pepper

BLACK BEAN SPARE RIBS

SERVES 4

The most common way to eat these ribs is as a type of dim sum, but they also make a great simple meaty meal served with some stir-fried pak choi and rice on the side. Traditionally, sodium bicarbonate and water are used to tenderize the meat, but I have found that leaving the ribs in the marinade overnight and steaming them for a longer period of time works just as well, with the benefit of retaining the natural texture of the meat.

1
Put the ribs into a large mixing bowl, add the marinade ingredients and, using your hands, massage them into the ribs until evenly coated. Cover and leave to marinate in the fridge for at least 1 hour, preferably overnight.

2
When you are ready to cook, transfer the marinated ribs to a heatproof plate that will fit in your bamboo steamer basket and sprinkle over half of the red chilli. Put the plate of ribs inside the basket, cover with the lid and place over a wok half-filled with boiling water. Steam for at least 20 minutes, or until the ribs are tender and light brown in colour (see Tip).

3
Remove the plate from the steamer, scatter the spring onion and remaining red chilli over the ribs to garnish and serve.

TIP To check that the ribs are properly cooked, look at the ends of the bones – if they are dark in colour with no red present, then the ribs are ready.

STEAMING

PREP 30 minutes

COOK 1¼ hours

400g (14oz) pork belly, with skin
1 sweet potato, peeled and cut into 5mm (¼ inch) thick slices
vegetable oil
3 spring onions, finely sliced
1 thumb-sized piece of ginger, peeled and finely sliced

SAUCE

4 tablespoons Shaoxing rice wine (swapsies: dry sherry)
2 tablespoons hoisin sauce
2 tablespoons light soy sauce
2 teaspoons dark soy sauce

KAMPO'S PORK BELLY & SWEET POTATO WITH HOISIN SPRING ONION SAUCE

SERVES 4

I first met Chef Kampo when I was searching for my own next cookery lesson. I wanted to learn how to make hand-pulled noodles, but running School of Wok made it difficult to find the time. Someone introduced me to Chef Kampo, an expert in Chinese cooking who has since become my go-to mentor for food advice. He suggested this recipe for this book, which you would never find in Chinese restaurants in the West but it is real home cooking. Even after spending over 35 years in professional kitchens, his home palate is just as humble, warming and generous as the man himself. This will satisfy and comfort on a cold winter night – true home-style Chinese cooking at its best.

1

Bring a large saucepan of water to the boil, add the pork belly and blanch for 10 minutes. Remove from the pan and cool under cold running water, then drain and cut into 1cm (½ inch) thick slices.

2

Mix the sauce ingredients together in a bowl.

3

Arrange the pork belly and sweet potato slices, one by one, alternately across a heatproof plate that will fit in your wok on a steamer stand – much like stacking CDs along a shelf (if you are old enough to know what a CD is!) – until you have used up all the pork.

4

Heat 1–2 tablespoons of vegetable oil in the wok over a medium heat. Add the spring onions and ginger and stir-fry for 1 minute until everything is aromatic and the spring onions are starting to brown. Pour in the sauce and bring to the boil, then reduce to a simmer and cook for 1–2 minutes until it has reduced by about a third. Pour over the layered pork and sweet potato.

5

Set the wok up with a steamer stand and fill with boiling water to halfway up the sides. Place the layered pork and sweet potato plate in the wok, cover with a lid and steam for about 1 hour until the sweet potato and pork pieces are fragrant and tender. Remove from the wok and serve.

TIP Because this recipe involves such a long period of steaming, check the water every 10 minutes to make sure the wok hasn't run dry, adding a little extra hot water if necessary.

SINGAPOREAN CHICKEN IN GINGER & GARLIC PASTE

SERVES 2

PREP 20 minutes, plus cooling
COOK 40 minutes

The slow cooked ginger and garlic paste of this dish is fried in a blend of sesame oil and vegetable oil, where low and slow cooking keeps the sesame oil from overheating, whilst creating a uniquely savoury flavour. You'd think that using this much ginger and garlic for one dish would be incredibly pungent, but cooking these strong base ingredients in this way for such a long time brings out their natural sweetness and removes their intensity completely.

- 300g (10½oz) skinless, boneless chicken thighs, cut into 2-3cm (¾-1¼ inch) dice or rough chunks
- 2 tablespoons sesame oil
- 1 tablespoon vegetable oil
- 1 spring onion, finely sliced into rings, to garnish

MARINADE

- 1½ tablespoons Shaoxing rice wine (swapsies: dry sherry)
- 1 tablespoon light soy sauce
- ½ teaspoon salt
- ½ teaspoon sugar
- ½ tablespoon cornflour

PASTE

- 200g (7oz) ginger, peeled and roughly chopped
- 2 heads of garlic, cloves separated and peeled
- 2 tablespoons sesame oil
- 1½ tablespoons oyster sauce
- ½ tablespoon light soy sauce
- ½ teaspoon sugar

TO SERVE

- steamed rice
- crunchy vegetables, such as any of the greens on pages 198–202

1 Put the chicken into a mixing bowl, add the marinade ingredients and, using your hands, massage them into the chicken pieces until evenly coated.

2 Transfer the marinated chicken to a heatproof plate that will fit in your wok or steamer pan on a steamer stand, with at least a thumb's-width space between the edge of the plate and the pan sides all the way around, for easy access once cooked.

3 Blitz the paste ingredients together in a food processor until smooth.

4 Heat the sesame and vegetable oils in the wok over a low heat. Once the wok is hot, add the paste and fry for 15–20 minutes, stirring every minute or so to prevent the garlic from burning, until it has dried and you start to see the oil separate from the ginger and garlic. Remove from the heat and allow the paste to cool.

5 Using your hands, massage 1–2 tablespoons of the paste into the marinated chicken, then generously spoon the rest over the chicken.

6 Set the wok up with the steamer stand and fill with boiling water halfway up the sides. Place the chicken plate in the wok or pan, cover with a lid and steam for 20 minutes, or until the chicken is cooked through and tender. Remove from the pan, scatter over the spring onion rings to garnish and serve with steamed rice and crunchy veg on the side.

TIP A heatproof pasta plate would work well for steaming the chicken.

CHAPTER 4
POACHING & BRAISING

POACHING & BRAISING

THE VAST MAJORITY of Chinese cooking methods, like those that we have already touched on, tend to be incredibly quick ways of cooking. While these may be the most commonly used methods of cooking in restaurants and takeaways, prized for their quick-turnaround nature, Chinese home cooking also allows for slower processes like poaching and braising, and in good Chinese restaurants they are often the 'lost dishes' that are well worth ordering.

These techniques are great for creating different textures and flavours in your cooking, with both relying on hot, bubbling liquids surrounding the ingredients inside the cooking vessel as their main source of heat for cooking.

Poaching is an effective way of preserving an ingredient's natural flavour and texture, while the aim of braising is to infuse ingredients and their cooking liquid with additional and intense flavours over a long period of time.

POACHING

A STEP-BY-STEP GUIDE

Poaching or 'soft boiling' is a very time-sensitive cooking method – think about the difference between hard-boiling or soft-boiling an egg, for instance. If you know what texture you are aiming to produce from your main ingredient, it will directly reflect how long you poach it for. The usual way to poach something, whether in a wok or a saucepan, is to:

1

Fill your wok or saucepan with water or stock, either with added ingredients to flavour the water (such as ginger, spring onion, garlic or star anise or other spice) or without, depending on your recipe.

2

Add your ingredient for poaching to the water or stock and apply heat to the pan to seal in the flavour. (Note: Some ingredients seal better by placing them directly into boiling water or stock, whereas others turn out better if added to the unheated liquid. Continue to poach your ingredient until it is cooked through, following the specific recipe to begin with in order to understand cooking times.

BRAISING
A STEP-BY-STEP GUIDE

Braising is essentially a simple form of double-cooking, where the main ingredients are often sealed in a light coating of oil before liquid is added to the pan. This initial searing process helps the ingredients to retain their natural moisture and flavour. Over time, during the braising process, these flavours will begin to infuse into the liquid they are being cooked in, and vice versa, resulting in a flavoursome dish. Generally, braising methods follow these simple principles:

1
Heat 1–2 tablespoons of vegetable oil in a heavy-based saucepan or clay pot to medium heat. Add your spices or marinated meats.

2
Add a sauce, braising liquid or stock to the pan.

3
Bring to the boil, then reduce the heat and simmer for as long as the ingredients will stay intact.

SICHUAN-STYLE AUBERGINE

PREP 30 minutes
COOK 20 minutes

SERVES 2

Cooking aubergine can be a bit of a task; due to its sponge-like nature, it can turn out very oily or even rubbery if undercooked or sealed the wrong way. Here, the initial frying of the aubergine works in the same way as searing a piece of meat before a slow cook. Sealing each piece and then braising the aubergine enables it to absorb the flavours of the rich sauce more gradually while cooking through evenly.

2 Chinese aubergines (swapsies: 8–10 small Indian aubergines or 1 large aubergine)
vegetable oil
2 garlic cloves, finely chopped
1 birds' eye chilli, finely chopped
small handful of coriander, finely chopped, to garnish

SAUCE
100ml (3½floz) water
1 tablespoon rice vinegar
1 tablespoon hoisin or yellow bean sauce
1 tablespoon light soy sauce
dash of dark soy sauce
2 teaspoons sugar
½ teaspoon chilli bean paste

1
Cut the aubergines in half lengthways, then slice into 2cm (¾ inch) thick long batons or 5cm (2 inch) chunks (if using Indian aubergines, just cut in half lengthways). Put them into a mixing bowl and immediately pour over 1–2 tablespoons of vegetable oil. Mix together well.

2
Heat a dry frying pan over a medium heat. Add the aubergine pieces and fry, turning, for about 2–3 minutes until golden brown and charred (but not burned) on both sides. Remove from the heat and set aside.

3
Mix the sauce ingredients together in a bowl.

4
Build your wok clock. Start at 12 o'clock with the garlic and charred aubergines, followed by the birds' eye chilli and finally the sauce.

5
Heat 1 tablespoon of vegetable oil in a wok over a medium heat. Add the garlic and charred aubergines and stir-fry for another 2–3 minutes. Then add the chilli and immediately pour over the sauce. Bring to a vigorous boil, then reduce the heat to a gentle simmer and cook for 12–15 minutes over a low heat, stirring occasionally, until the sauce has caramelized and thickened slightly.

6
Spoon onto a serving plate, scatter over the coriander to garnish and serve.

MIXED MUSHROOM & TOFU STEW

SERVES 4

PREP 20 minutes, plus soaking

COOK 35 minutes

There are many different types of tofu available and, though generally similar in flavour, each offers a slightly different texture. By knowing which type best matches which style of cooking, you will be able to retain its unique texture while allowing it to absorb as much flavour as possible. Japanese egg tofu, for example, forms a fantastic golden-brown coating when fried due to its egg content, whereas rolled bean-curd skin or deep-fried tofu squares (known as tofu *pok*) are so absorbent that they will suck up the flavour of any sauce you cook them in within 5–10 minutes.

Ingredients

- vegetable oil
- 300g (10½oz) Japanese egg tofu, sliced into 2cm (¾ inch) cylinders
- 1 thumb-sized piece of ginger, peeled and sliced
- 1 star anise
- 12 dried shiitake mushrooms, soaked in hot water for at least 2 hours, preferably overnight, then drained and 300ml (10fl oz) of the soaking water reserved
- 2 tablespoons vegetarian oyster sauce
- 1 tablespoon Shaoxing rice wine (swapsies: dry sherry)
- dash of dark soy sauce
- 10 deep-fried tofu squares, halved
- 300g (10½oz) straw or oyster mushrooms, roughly torn into chunks
- 1 spring onion, finely sliced into rings, to garnish
- steamed rice, to serve

1
Heat 1 tablespoon of vegetable oil in a frying pan over a medium-high heat. Add the egg tofu pieces and fry for 2 minutes on each side, or until golden brown. Remove from the pan and drain on a clean tea towel.

2
Build your wok clock. Start at 12 o'clock with the ginger and star anise, followed by the soaked dried shiitake mushrooms, oyster sauce, Shaoxing rice wine, dark soy sauce and mushroom soaking water, deep-fried tofu and finally the fried egg tofu and fresh mushrooms.

3
Heat 1 tablespoon of vegetable oil in a saucepan or clay pot over a medium heat. Add the ginger and star anise and fry for 30 seconds until slightly fragrant. Add the soaked shiitake mushrooms and cook for 2–3 minutes, then add the oyster sauce and cook, stirring, for another 2–3 minutes until the sauce has thickened and caramelized. Pour over the rice wine, dark soy sauce and mushroom soaking water and bring to the boil, then reduce the heat to a simmer.

4
Add the deep-fried tofu to the wok and simmer for 10 minutes, stirring occasionally. Then add the fried egg tofu and fresh mushrooms and simmer for 5–10 minutes until the stew has thickened and reduced, the mushrooms have softened and the tofu has soaked up all the stew's flavours.

5
Remove from the heat, garnish with the spring onion and then serve with steamed rice.

TIP If the stew is watery after the cooking time, mix 2 teaspoons of cornflour and 1 tablespoon of cold water together to make a paste and stir it into the sauce over a rolling boil. Leave the stew to thicken, then remove from the heat.

PREP	COOK
10 minutes	40 minutes

1 onion, finely sliced

1 thumb-sized piece of ginger, peeled and cut into fine matchsticks

300g (10½oz) chicken thighs and/or legs, with skin and bone

pinch of Chinese five spice

about 300–500ml (10–18fl oz) hot (not boiling) water

vegetable oil

small handful of coriander leaves, roughly chopped, to garnish

SAUCE

6 tablespoons dark soy sauce

3 tablespoons sugar

SOY SAUCE CHICKEN

SERVES 2

This is one of the simplest chicken dishes that you can come across in the Chinese home kitchen – it's great for teaching to kids or young adults getting ready for university or leaving home for the first time. The key to it is to ensure you caramelize the soy sauce and sugar mixture well enough before you add the water to the chicken. With that in mind, the rest is simple: simply sear, stir and boil.

1

Mix the sauce ingredients together in a small bowl or ramekin.

2

Build your wok clock. Start at 12 o'clock with the onion and ginger, followed by the chicken pieces, five spice and sauce and finally the measured water.

3

Heat 1 tablespoon of vegetable oil in a saucepan over a medium heat. Add the onion and ginger and cook, stirring, for 2–3 minutes, or until the onion starts to brown.

4

Add the chicken pieces and fry for 4–5 minutes, turning over as necessary, until golden brown on all sides. Then add the five spice and sauce and bring to the boil, stirring well to dissolve the sugar. Reduce the heat to a simmer and cook for another 4–5 minutes until the sauce has thickened and caramelized, stirring to ensure the chicken pieces are evenly coated.

5

Add just enough of the measured hot water to cover the chicken pieces. Bring to the boil, then reduce the heat, cover the pan with a lid and simmer for 15 minutes, or until the chicken is cooked through and tender.

6

Remove the lid and continue to simmer for 10 minutes, stirring occasionally, until the sauce has reduced by half and is dark, sticky and caramelized. Transfer to a serving bowl or plate, garnish with the coriander and serve.

TIP Try adding a few greens here by throwing a bag of green beans or sugarsnaps into the pot 3 minutes before serving.

CURRIED SQUID

SERVES 2–3

PREP 20 minutes
COOK 1–1¾ hours

We are so used to seeing squid fried or grilled that many might find the idea of this dish a bit strange. Trust me, take the leap of faith and make it – I promise you won't regret it. Although curries are by no means a Chinese delicacy, this slow-braised squid can be found bubbling away all day in the streets of Hong Kong, where there has been a significant Indian community for many years. The Cantonese have added their own twist to it by sweetening it up with evaporated milk and sugar. Again, this might sound odd, but this kind of sweet-savoury balance tastes delicious! Serve alongside something hot and crispy like the Shiitake & Chive Dumplings (see page 82) or some crusty French bread for dipping into the sauce.

- 1 tablespoon Madras curry powder
- ½ teaspoon ground turmeric
- 1 tablespoon sesame oil
- 300ml (10fl oz) chicken stock
- 100ml (3½fl oz) evaporated milk
- 1 teaspoon salt
- ½ tablespoon sugar
- 6 Thai shallots, finely diced
- 4 garlic cloves, finely diced
- 1 teaspoon cumin seeds
- 1 small cinnamon stick
- 10 fresh curry leaves (optional)
- 20 baby squid, cleaned and quills removed (ask the fishmonger to do this for you)
- vegetable oil
- crusty bread, to serve

1
Mix the curry powder, turmeric and sesame oil together in a small bowl or ramekin to form a paste.
Mix together the stock, evaporated milk, salt and sugar in a jug or bowl.

2
Build your wok clock. Start at 12 o'clock with the Thai shallots, followed by the garlic, cumin seeds and cinnamon stick, curry leaves, if using, and curry paste, squid and finally the stock and evaporated milk mixture.

3
Heat 2 tablespoons of vegetable oil in a saucepan over a medium heat. Add the Thai shallots and cook, stirring occasionally, for 6–8 minutes until softened. Then add the garlic, cumin seeds and cinnamon stick and cook, stirring, for 2–3 minutes, or until the cumin seeds start to brown. Add the curry leaves, if using, and curry paste and cook for another minute.

4
Add the squid to the pan and fry in the spices for 1–2 minutes. Pour over the stock and evaporated milk mixture and bring to the boil, then reduce to a gentle simmer, cover the pan with a lid and cook for at least 45 minutes (or up to 1½ hours) over a low heat. The sauce will have thickened slightly but should still have a brothy consistency. Serve with crusty French bread on the side.

PREP
20 minutes, plus marinating

COOK
3¾–4¾ hours

BEEF BRISKET NOODLE SOUP

SERVES 2–3

Beef brisket noodle soup is a classic midnight feast in southern China. The best time to eat this is late at night, after the beef has been cooking away in its fragrant, thick broth since the morning and it's so succulent that you won't be able to resist it. So the longer you are able to braise this at home, the better it will taste.

300g (10½oz) beef brisket or shin, cut into 2cm (¾ inch) cubes

1 thumb-sized piece of ginger, peeled and finely sliced

3 spring onions, sliced into wedges

1.5–2 litres (2⅔–3½ pints) water

½ daikon, peeled and chopped into chunks (swapsies: turnip or any radish)

100g (3½oz) dried thin egg noodles

extra spring onion, finely shredded, to garnish

leafy greens, such as pak choi, choi sum or Chinese broccoli (*kai lan*), to serve

MARINADE

1 tablespoon light soy sauce

1 tablespoon oyster sauce

1 tablespoon yellow bean sauce

1 tablespoon Shaoxing rice wine (swapsies: dry sherry)

1 teaspoon sesame oil

½ teaspoon Chinese five spice

½ teaspoon sugar

STOCK

500ml (18fl oz) chicken stock

3 tablespoons light soy sauce

2½ teaspoons salt

WHOLE SPICES

3–4 bay leaves

3 star anise

1 cinnamon stick

1
Put the beef into a mixing bowl. Add the marinade ingredients and, using your hands, massage them into the beef pieces until they are evenly coated. Cover and leave to marinate in the fridge for at least 1 hour, preferably overnight.
Mix the stock ingredients together in a jug or bowl.

2
Build your wok clock. Start at 12 o'clock with the whole spices, followed by the ginger, spring onions and stock, the marinated beef, daikon and finally the noodles.

3
Heat a large dry saucepan over a medium heat. Add the spices and heat them through for 2–3 minutes until aromatic. Then add the ginger, spring onions and stock as well as the measured water. Bring to a rolling boil. Add the beef, then reduce the heat, cover the pan with a lid and simmer for 3–4 hours over a low heat until the meat is completely tender and beginning to fall apart.

4
Add the daikon and bring the stock back to a rolling boil, then reduce the heat to a simmer and cook for another 30 minutes.

5
Meanwhile, soak the noodles in hot water for 3–4 minutes until they have separated. Drain and leave to dry on a clean tea towel for 10 minutes, or until you are ready to serve.

6
Blanch the noodles in the stock for 30 seconds–1 minute and then divide the noodles between serving bowls. Briefly poach the leafy greens in the soup for 1 minute and place on top of the noodles. Lastly, ladle a portion of beef and daikon, and the soup, over each serving of noodles and greens. Then scatter over the spring onion to garnish.

TIP To reduce the cooking time, you can use a pressure cooker, if you have one, to cook the beef mixture for 30–45 minutes on a high pressure function, then for a final 5–10 minutes after adding the daikon.

PREP
45 minutes

COOK
50 minutes–1 hour

250g (9oz) white crabmeat

200g (7oz) minced pork

100g (3½oz) raw prawns, peeled and deveined (see Tip, page 94), then finely diced

100g (3½oz) water chestnuts, finely diced

1 thumb-sized piece of ginger, peeled and finely diced

2 spring onions, finely diced

vegetable oil, for deep-frying

large handful of coriander, roughly chopped, to garnish

steamed rice, to serve

MARINADE

2 tablespoons water

1 tablespoon light soy sauce

1½ tablespoons cornflour

2 teaspoons sesame oil

½ teaspoon salt

½ teaspoon black pepper

SAUCE

1 thumb-sized piece of ginger, peeled and finely sliced

1 head of Chinese leaf, cut into 3cm (1¼ inch) squares

1½ tablespoons oyster sauce

300ml (10fl oz) chicken stock

GRANDMA'S 'LIONHEAD' MEATBALLS

SERVES 4

There are some things we miss dearly from the days when Grandma Pang was alive. Most of them (as tends to be the case with our family) food related. These *see ji tau* or 'lionhead' meatballs with their unique texture and comforting flavours are one of her stand-out dishes. Grandma only ever made them in massive quantities – it was as though, when cooking them, she couldn't quite figure out when to stop, worried that someone might be a bit hungrier than she had planned. Whatever the reason, this warming, winter one-pot wonder is something I recommend cooking enough of for everyone to have at least seconds, if not thirds.

1

Put the crabmeat, minced pork, prawns, water chestnuts, ginger and spring onions into a large mixing bowl, add the marinade ingredients and, using your hands, mix together, then beat to form a smooth paste (see Tip, page 116).

2

Fill a bowl with cold water. Dip the palms of your hands into the water, then pick up and roll a portion of the meatball mixture into ping-pong-sized balls. Repeat with the rest of the meat mixture, then place the meatballs on a large cold plate.

3

Half-fill a large pot, wok or deep-fryer with vegetable oil and heat to 180°C/350°F, or until the tip of a wooden chopstick or skewer starts to fizz after 2–3 seconds in the oil. Deep-fry the meatballs, in batches, for 4 minutes until golden brown. Remove with a slotted spoon and drain well on a plate lined with kitchen paper.

4

For the sauce, heat 1 tablespoon of vegetable oil in a saucepan over a medium heat. Add the ginger and Chinese leaf and stir-fry for 2–3 minutes. Then add the oyster sauce and stock and bring to the boil.

5

Reduce the heat to a simmer and carefully lower the meatballs into the sauce. Cover the pan with a lid and simmer for 30–40 minutes until the sauce has thickened by half. Spoon the meatballs and sauce into serving bowls, garnish with the coriander and serve with steamed rice.

PREP
30 minutes

COOK
2¼ hours

4 eggs, hard-boiled, cooled and shelled

600g (1lb 5oz) pork belly, with skin, halved (if the ribs are still attached then keep them in)

2 garlic cloves, finely chopped

1 thumb-sized piece of ginger, peeled and bashed

3–4 spring onions, roughly chopped

about 450ml (16fl oz) hot water

vegetable oil

SAUCE

2 cubes of red fermented tofu, plus 2 tablespoons fermented tofu liquid

2 tablespoons dark soy sauce

1 tablespoon Chinkiang vinegar (swapsies: rice vinegar)

1 tablespoon sugar

PORK BELLY IN FERMENTED TOFU

SERVES 4

Ingredients like fermented tofu and eggs provide a great way of thickening sauces without the use of cornflour. The fermented red tofu used here has a powerfully salty flavour if eaten alone, which is very much an acquired taste. However, when it's made into a paste and cooked into this braising liquid, it adds a silky finish to the sauce and gives it a real depth of flavour. If you can't find it, make a paste out of one of the hard-boiled egg yolks, which will thicken the sauce much like the tofu does. This dish, a favourite of my dad's, is a family meal we had often – its intense flavour is perfect paired with rice and something light and fresh like the Flash-fried Morning Glory (see page 198) or Pickled Lotus Root & Spinach (see page 206).

1

For the sauce, put the fermented tofu and liquid into a small bowl or ramekin and crush with the back of a teaspoon to form a paste, then mix together with the rest of the sauce ingredients.

Cut 3 small lines vertically into each hard-boiled egg while keeping them whole (this allows the sauce to soak through the eggs).

2

Build your wok clock. Start at 12 o'clock with the pork, followed by the garlic, ginger and spring onions, the sauce, measured hot water and finally the boiled eggs.

3

Heat 1 tablespoon of vegetable oil in a large saucepan over a high heat. Add the pork, skin-side down, and sear for 3–4 minutes until golden brown, then turn and sear each side. Add the garlic, ginger and spring onions and cook, stirring, for 30 seconds until the spring onions are lightly browned. Pour over the sauce and bring to the boil, then reduce the heat and simmer for 5 minutes, basting the pork in the caramelizing sauce around the meat.

4

Once the sauce is thick and coating the meat well, turn the pork skin-side up and pour over enough of the measured hot water to cover it completely. Stir everything together well, cover the pan with a lid and simmer over a low heat for at least 1½ hours, turning the pork occasionally, until it is soft, succulent and full of colour.

5

Remove the lid, add the eggs to the braising liquid and simmer for another 30 minutes, turning the eggs every 10 minutes to ensure they absorb the sauce evenly. Arrange on a large serving platter and serve.

PREP
30 minutes, plus soaking

COOK
15 minutes

2 garlic cloves, unpeeled

300g (10½oz) cod fillet, skin on and descaled, diagonally sliced into 1cm (½ inch) thick slices

1 thumb-sized piece of ginger, peeled and finely sliced

2 spring onions, cut into 3cm (1¼ inch) pieces

½ carrot, finely sliced

½ celery stick, peeled and cut into 3cm (1¼ inch) pieces

handful of dried wood ear mushrooms, soaked in hot water for at least 2 hours, preferably overnight, then drained

300ml (10fl oz) fish or chicken stock

vegetable oil

salt and black pepper

steamed rice, to serve

MARINADE

1 egg white, beaten

½ tablespoon cornflour

2 teaspoons sesame oil

½ teaspoon salt

½ teaspoon sugar

COD FILLET WITH WOOD EAR MUSHROOM & SPRING ONION BROTH

SERVES 2

Poaching is such a wonderful way to cook fish. The idea behind poaching cod fillet in a light and earthy broth like this is to keep it soft and delicate, while accentuating the flavour of the fish itself. The carrot and celery add colour, while the wood ear mushrooms provide a great contrasting texture to the flaky white fish.

1

Using the flat side of a knife or cleaver, smash the garlic cloves to release their flavour, but don't peel or discard the skin.

Put the cod into a mixing bowl. Add the marinade ingredients and, using your hands, gently massage them into the fish pieces until evenly coated.

2

Build your wok clock. Start at 12 o'clock with the smashed garlic cloves, followed by the ginger and spring onions, carrot, celery and soaked dried wood ear mushrooms, stock and finally the marinated cod.

3

Heat 1½ tablespoons of vegetable oil in a wok over a low heat. Add the smashed garlic cloves and cook for 4–5 minutes, turning occasionally, until the skins start to brown.

4

Increase the heat to medium-high, add the ginger and spring onions to the wok and stir-fry for 1 minute until fragrant and lightly browned. Then add the carrot, celery and soaked dried wood ear mushrooms and stir-fry for 2–3 minutes.

5

Pour in the stock and bring to a vigorous boil, then carefully add the fish pieces, reduce the heat to a medium simmer and cook for 3 minutes until the fish is white and opaque all the way through. Season with salt and black pepper to taste, then serve with steamed rice.

TIP Keeping the skin on the garlic in this recipe helps protect it from burning in the pan, while the slow cooking allows its flavours to gradually infuse into the oil. Finely chopped garlic would burn very quickly if cooked this way.

PREP	COOK
25 minutes, plus soaking	40–50 minutes

500g (1lb 2oz) boneless pork shoulder

½ thumb-sized piece of ginger, peeled and roughly chopped

3 garlic cloves, roughly chopped

2 spring onions, roughly chopped

10 dried shiitake mushrooms, soaked in hot water for at least 2 hours, preferably overnight, then drained and 200ml (7fl oz) of the soaking water reserved, mushrooms quartered

200ml (7fl oz) chicken stock

vegetable oil

steamed jasmine rice, to serve

SAUCE

2 tablespoons Shaoxing rice wine (swapsies: dry sherry)

1½ tablespoons dark soy sauce

1 tablespoon light soy sauce

1 tablespoon oyster sauce

1 tablespoon soft brown sugar

WHOLE SPICES

5 bay leaves

2 star anise

1 teaspoon fennel seeds

TAIWANESE BRAISED PORK RICE

SERVES 4

Here is a simpler, quicker version of the Pork Belly in Fermented Tofu on page 154, based on the Taiwanese rustic dish *lu rou fan*, where the earthy nature of shiitake mushrooms is used to accentuate the flavours. Like a good curry, I think this dish tastes better the next day. If you can wait that long, you could also marinate some soft-boiled eggs, after cooling and shelling, in the braising liquid and flash-fry some greens on the side for an extremely satisfying meal.

1

Place the pork in the centre of a chopping board. Hold the tip of a cleaver with your crab hand (see pages 18 and 21). Rock the cleaver up and down in a fast rocking motion and run the blade up and down the piece of meat lightly, taking care not to cut completely through it. This will make lots of little cuts across the meat, opening up the surface area to allow as much of the marinade to penetrate as possible. Slice the pork into strips.

Mix the sauce ingredients together in a small bowl.

2

Build your wok clock. Start at 12 o'clock with the ginger, garlic and spring onions, followed by the whole spices, marinated pork, soaked dried shiitake mushrooms, sauce and finally the stock and mushroom soaking water.

3

Heat 1 tablespoon of vegetable oil in a heavy-based wok or saucepan over a medium heat. Add the ginger, garlic and spring onions and stir-fry for 1 minute until the ginger and garlic are well browned. Then add the whole spices and stir-fry for 30–60 seconds. Add the pork and sear for 3–4 minutes, folding occasionally, until the edges are all browned and slightly crisp.

4

Increase the heat to high, add the soaked dried shiitake mushrooms and stir-fry for 2–3 minutes, then pour in the sauce and bring to a vigorous boil. Reduce the heat to medium and bubble away for 5 minutes, folding the sauce into the pork every minute or so.

5

Pour the stock and mushroom soaking water into the wok, reduce the heat to medium-low and simmer for 20–30 minutes until the sauce has started to thicken and become more syrupy in texture. Heap the braised pork and sauce over the cooked jasmine rice and serve.

PREP
25 minutes, plus standing

COOK
45 minutes

1.5kg (3lb 5oz) whole chicken
½ teaspoon salt
3 tablespoons light soy sauce
1 tablespoon dark soy sauce
2 tablespoons sesame oil
1 teaspoon sugar
1 thumb-sized piece of ginger, peeled and finely sliced
3 spring onions, roughly chopped
6 garlic cloves, smashed and peeled
300ml (10fl oz) chicken stock
250g (9oz) jasmine rice, rinsed
vegetable oil
½ cucumber, finely sliced, to serve

CHILLI SAUCE

½ thumb-sized piece of ginger, peeled and roughly chopped
4 garlic cloves, roughly chopped
10 large red chillies, halved
3 tablespoons rice vinegar
3 tablespoons hot vegetable stock
1 teaspoon sesame oil
1 teaspoon salt
½ teaspoon sugar

GINGER OIL

3 spring onions, finely chopped
1 large knob of ginger, peeled and finely chopped
¼ teaspoon salt
2 tablespoons vegetable oil

HAINANESE CHICKEN RICE WITH GINGER OIL

SERVES 6

I first tried this dish when I was ten years old at a stall in a hawker centre in Singapore, not Hainan. One mouthful transformed me from being a picky eater to an adventurous and engaged one like the rest of my family. Cooked well, this dish is sure to make anyone's mouth water.

1

Cut the parson's nose off your chicken and rub the chicken all over with the salt.

Blitz all the chilli sauce ingredients together in a food processor, then pour the sauce into a saucepan. Bring to the boil over a medium heat and cook until the sugar has melted. Allow to cool. (Once cooled, you can store the sauce, covered, in the fridge for up to 2–3 days.)

Mix the soy sauces, sesame oil and sugar together in a small bowl or ramekin until dissolved.

2

Build your wok clock. Start at 12 o'clock with the ginger, spring onions and smashed garlic, followed by the stock, chicken, rice, sesame soy sauce mixture and finally the ginger oil ingredients.

3

Heat 1 tablespoon of vegetable oil in a large saucepan over a medium heat. Add the ginger, spring onions and smashed garlic and stir-fry for 2–3 minutes until the garlic and ginger are crisp and golden brown. Pour in the stock, lower in the chicken and cover with cold water until fully submerged. Cover the pan with a lid and bring to the boil, then reduce the heat and simmer for 20 minutes.

4

Remove the pan from the heat and leave the covered pot for 40 minutes. Check the chicken is cooked through by poking a small, sharp paring knife through the thickest part, the juices should run clear. Carefully remove the chicken from the pan, reserving the poaching liquid, and submerge it in a pan of cold water for 2 minutes. Drain and then baste it in the sauce. Set aside for 20 minutes.

5

Put the rice in a saucepan with 320ml (11fl oz) of the poaching liquid. Mix together, cover with a lid and bring to a rolling boil over a high heat, then reduce the heat and simmer for 10 minutes. Turn the heat off and leave to steam with the lid on for 15 minutes.

6

For the ginger oil, mix the spring onions, ginger and salt in a heatproof bowl. Heat the vegetable oil in a small pan until smoking hot, then pour over the mix to sizzle and mix.

7

Carve the chicken and arrange it on a large serving platter with the ginger oil and chicken rice, then serve along with the cucumber and chilli sauce.

PREP	COOK
20 minutes	30 minutes

SICHUAN BOILED FISH

SERVES 4

River fish is a lot more prominent in Chinese cuisine than in the West and features in the traditional dish (*shui zhu yu*), but you can use any firm white fish fillets here. The thin slices allow for a quick poach or blanch in the flavourful stock, finishing with sizzling chilli oil poured over the hot liquid, a technique unique to Sichuan cooking that leaves a coating of spicy oil around each piece of fish when fished out with chopsticks.

500g (1lb 2oz) white fish fillets (such as carp, sea bass, bream or cod), with skin, diagonally cut into thin slices

½ thumb-sized piece of ginger, peeled and roughly chopped

3 garlic cloves, roughly chopped

3 large red chillies, roughly chopped

100g (3½oz) pickled mustard greens (*za cai*), roughly chopped (swapsies: sauerkraut or gherkins)

1½ tablespoons chilli bean paste

vegetable oil

handful of coriander, leaves picked, to garnish

500ml (18fl oz) chicken stock

1 tablespoon light soy sauce

1 teaspoon salt

½ teaspoon sugar

MARINADE

½ teaspoon salt

¼ teaspoon sugar

1 tablespoon Shaoxing rice wine (swapsies: dry sherry)

1 egg white, beaten

1 tablespoon cornflour

CHILLI OIL

2–3 tablespoons vegetable oil

3 garlic cloves, roughly chopped

handful of dried red chillies, roughly chopped

1 teaspoon Sichuan peppercorns

1

Put the fish into a mixing bowl. Add the salt, sugar and Shaoxing rice wine for the marinade and massage into the fish slices. Then add the egg white and massage it in, followed by the cornflour and repeat until everything is well combined.

Mix the chicken stock, light soy sauce, salt and sugar together in a large jug or bowl.

For the chilli oil, heat the vegetable oil in a small saucepan over a low-medium heat. Add the garlic, dried red chillies and Sichuan peppercorns, slowly stir them into the oil and fry for 1–2 minutes. Set aside.

2

Build your wok clock. Start at 12 o'clock with the ginger, garlic and red chillies, followed by the pickled mustard greens, chilli bean paste, stock, marinated fish and finally the chilli oil.

3

Heat 2 tablespoons of vegetable oil in a wok over a medium-high heat. Add the ginger, garlic and red chillies and stir-fry for 1–2 minutes until the ginger and garlic turn golden brown and start to crisp up. Then add the pickled mustard greens and stir-fry for a minute or so. Add the chilli bean paste and stir-fry for 1 minute.

4

Pour the stock into the wok, bring to the boil and continue boiling for 15 minutes, then turn off the heat. Immediately add the marinated fish and allow to sit in the hot stock for 1–2 minutes. Reheat the stock until vigorously boiling, then reduce the heat to a low simmer for 1 minute.

5

Just before serving, reheat the chilli oil over a medium-high heat for 30–60 seconds and pour over the top of the soup to finish. Garnish with the coriander leaves and serve immediately.

YUNNAN LITTLE POT RICE NOODLES

SERVES 2

PREP	COOK
10 minutes, plus soaking & drying	45 minutes

I do wonder whether the idea of pot noodles came from Yunnan, home of the famous Crossing the Bridge Noodles, involving a large pot of boiling water into which many little dishes of ingredients are progressively fed. I sometimes fancifully think that if you were a tiny human, you could jump into one pot, have a little swim and a bite to eat, then cross the bridge to the next pot of noodle heaven. This one-pot noodle wonder is a much simpler concept and yet just as tasty, holding intense flavours from the pickles and the fermented bean paste, balanced by the sweetness of the soy sauce.

150g (5½oz) dried Jiangxi rice vermicelli sticks (thick rice vermicelli noodles) (swapsies: dried rice vermicelli or flat rice noodles)

100g (3½oz) pickled mustard greens (*za cai*), roughly chopped (swapsies: gherkins or capers)

¼ teaspoon Chinese five spice

½ teaspoon chilli powder

vegetable oil

3 star anise

2–3 black cardamom pods

handful of Chinese chives (swapsies: spring onions or green beans, cut into matchsticks)

100g (3½oz) beansprouts, rinsed

BEAN PASTE

1 tablespoon preserved fermented black beans

1 tablespoon chilli bean paste

¼ teaspoon chilli powder

SWEET SOY

3 tablespoons dark soy sauce

1 tablespoon brown sugar

STOCK

1 litre (1¾ pints) chicken stock

1 tablespoon light soy sauce

½ teaspoon salt

1

Soak the noodles in hot water for 8–10 minutes until they have separated. Drain and leave to dry on a clean tea towel until you are ready to use them.

Mix the pickled mustard greens with the Chinese five spice and chilli powder in a mixing bowl. Heat 1 tablespoon of vegetable oil in a wok over a medium heat. Add the mustard greens and stir-fry for 2–3 minutes to temper the spices. Remove from the wok and set aside.

For the bean paste, pound the preserved fermented black beans using a pestle and mortar to form a thick paste, then add the chilli bean paste and chilli powder and mix well. Heat 1 tablespoon of vegetable oil in the wok over a medium heat. Add the bean paste and stir-fry for 1–2 minutes until thickened. Remove from the wok and set aside.

Mix the sweet soy ingredients together in the wok. Bring to the boil over a medium heat and cook until the sugar has fully dissolved, then remove from the wok and set aside.

Mix the stock ingredients together in a jug or bowl.

2

Build your wok clock. Start at 12 o'clock with the star anise and black cardamoms, followed by the stock, spiced pickled mustard greens, bean paste, sweet soy, noodles, Chinese chives and finally the beansprouts.

3

Heat a dry saucepan over a medium heat. Add the star anise and black cardamoms and heat for 1–2 minutes until aromatic. Pour in the stock and bring to the boil, then reduce the heat and simmer for 5 minutes.

4

Add the spiced pickled mustard greens and simmer for 30 seconds, then add the bean paste and simmer for 30 seconds, followed by the sweet soy. Continue to simmer for 15–20 minutes to allow the flavours to infuse together into the stock.

5

A few minutes before serving, add the noodles to the stock and simmer for 1 minute, then add the Chinese chives and beansprouts, simmering for 1 minute after each addition. Serve immediately.

PREP
20 minutes

COOK
45 minutes

4 whole chicken legs (thigh and drumstick), with skin and bone, chopped into 4–5cm (1½–2 inch) chunks (ask the butcher to do this for you)

2 thumb-sized pieces of ginger, peeled, thickly sliced and bashed

4 garlic cloves, roughly chopped

300ml (10fl oz) chicken stock

100g (3½oz) peeled chestnuts

3 large green chillies, roughly chopped

3 large red chillies, roughly chopped

vegetable oil

MARINADE

1 tablespoon Shaoxing rice wine (swapsies: dry sherry)

½ teaspoon salt

SAUCE

1 tablespoon Shaoxing rice wine (swapsies: dry sherry)

½ tablespoon light soy sauce

½ tablespoon dark soy sauce

WHOLE SPICES

5–6 dried red chillies

3 star anise

2–3 black cardamom pods, cracked

1 teaspoon black or red peppercorns

YONG PING YELLOW CHICKEN

SERVES 4

Chestnuts and black cardamom are both quite obscure ingredients that are perhaps not associated with Chinese cuisine in the West. Their earthy nature brings this half braised, half stir-fried chicken to life, and changing the heat up and down to break the chestnuts down creates an almost creamy, savoury, irresistible sauce.

1

Put the chicken into a mixing bowl. Add the marinade ingredients and, using your hands, massage them into the chicken pieces until well combined.

Mix the sauce ingredients together in a small bowl or ramekin.

2

Build your wok clock. Start at 12 o'clock with the marinated chicken, followed by the whole spices, the ginger and garlic, stock, chestnuts, green and red chillies and finally the sauce.

3

Heat 2–3 tablespoons of vegetable oil in a wok over a high heat until smoking hot. Add the chicken and sear for 5–6 minutes until the skin is golden brown and crispy around the edges. Then add the whole spices and stir-fry for 1–2 minutes. Add the ginger and garlic and stir-fry for 2 minutes.

4

Pour the stock into the wok and bring to a vigorous boil. Add the chestnuts and reduce the heat to a medium simmer. Cover the wok with a lid and simmer for 15 minutes until the chicken and chestnuts are cooked through.

5

Remove the lid, increase the heat to high and cook for 5–10 minutes until the liquid has reduced by half. Then add the green and red chillies and cook, stirring, for 1–2 minutes.

6

Pour in the sauce to season the dish and fold through, then serve.

CHAPTER 5
ROASTING & DOUBLE-COOKING

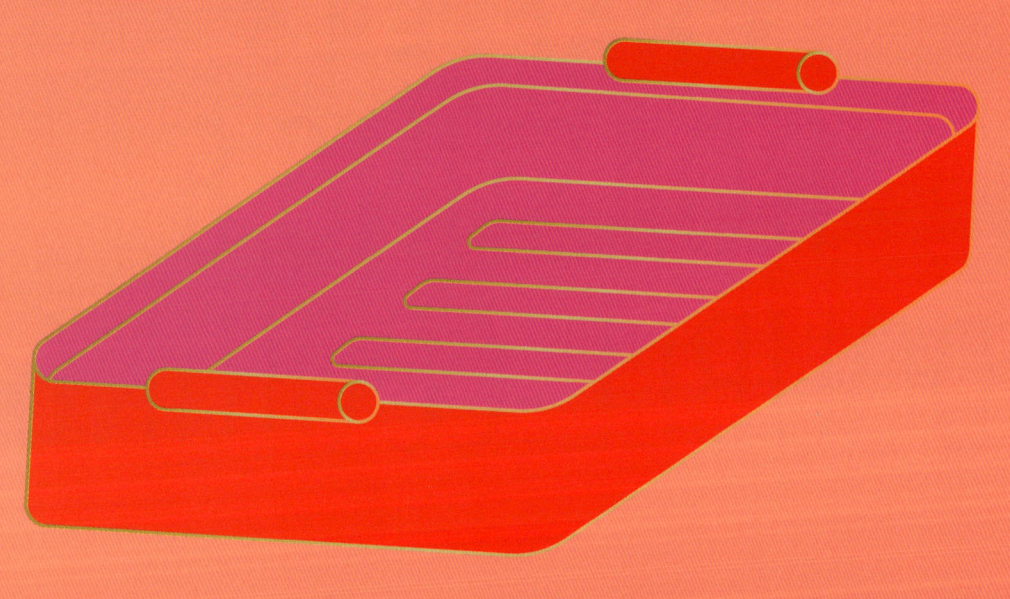

ROASTING & DOUBLE-COOKING

WHILE ROASTING and double-cooking play big parts in Chinese cuisine, they can feel overwhelming or time-consuming. This chapter is my ultimate tribute to the slow-cooking process. The recipes are not necessarily difficult, but they require a patience that doesn't always align well with the bustle of modern life. These are recipes to be tackled on a quiet weekend, and the results are worth waiting for.

While traditional Chinese ovens are hard to come by today, most restaurants used to have a large walk-in clay oven. This would have a huge chimney in the middle of its roof and small wind tunnels built into the walls to allow air to circulate through the oven itself – the thick clay walls would hold in the heat while the meat would be hung along the inside walls, with coal pits underneath creating the heat for the slow-cooked, 'wind-dried' style of cooking. It allowed the outside skin to char away while the meat would slowly roast until succulent and tender, creating a crispy skin and melt-in-the-mouth meat. These days restaurants use stainless-steel ovens that do a very similar job and, though it can be difficult to replicate such a unique cooking environment at home, there are ways and means of creating similar outcomes with a domestic oven.

Double-cooking is precisely that: combining two or more basic techniques from this book to cook one dish. As a balance of textures is so important in Chinese food, the Chinese love to use double-cooking processes to give different textures to meat, seafood and even certain vegetable dishes. There are no specific rules for double-cooking, though there are some general guidelines as to how to order the cooking techniques to ensure a successful outcome (blanching, poaching, deep-frying or braising tend to come first, while the second or third processes are more likely to be roasting, stir-frying, or steaming). Sometimes a dish may use up to four or five different cooking techniques. The typical dim sum, chickens' feet, is one example: to give the skin its signature melt-in-the-mouth feel, the feet are blanched, then dried, then deep-fried, then braised, then marinated and finally steamed to finish. This may seem excessive, but it's an amazing way to make something seemingly tasteless take in so much flavour. There is method in the madness!

PREP
25 minutes,
plus soaking

COOK
20 minutes

100g (3½oz) skinless cod fillet or other white fish fillet, cut into rough pieces

200g (7oz) raw prawns, peeled and deveined (see Tip, page 94)

large pinch of salt

large pinch of black pepper

2 spring onions, finely chopped

large handful of coriander, finely chopped, plus extra to garnish

1 garlic clove, finely chopped

1 large aubergine

2 red peppers, cut into large wedges, seeds discarded and cores intact

3 tablespoons cornflour

vegetable oil

salt

SAUCE

150ml (5fl oz) chicken stock

1 tablespoon oyster sauce

½ tablespoon light soy sauce

½ teaspoon sugar

1 thumb-sized piece of ginger, peeled and finely chopped

SEAFOOD-STUFFED ROAST PEPPERS & AUBERGINES

SERVES 4

This classic Cantonese dish is often made using a filling of dace, a paste of small fish that can be bought locally. Unfortunately, it is not easy to find this luxury outside of Canton, so to mimic the paste's texture I use a combination of blended prawns and fish – the fish providing softness, while the prawns give bite. With the speedy sauce, this makes for a great quick and easy dinner.

1
Preheat the oven to 200°C/425°F/Gas Mark 7.

2
Mix together all the sauce ingredients except the ginger in a bowl.

3
Put the fish and prawns into a food processor and blitz together gradually, seasoning with the salt and black pepper as you go, until a thick paste forms. Transfer the mixture to a mixing bowl, add the spring onions, coriander and garlic and mix everything together well.

4
Cut the aubergine diagonally into 3cm (1¼ inch) thick slices, then slice each piece through the skin three-quarters of the way through without cutting the pieces in half, effectively making a sandwich, with a pocket for the filling. Put the aubergine pieces into a large bowl filled with salted water and set aside for 30 minutes or so.

5
Drain the aubergine pieces and pat them dry with kitchen paper. Dust the inside of the aubergine 'sandwiches' and the red pepper wedges with the cornflour, then stuff them all with the fish mixture. Place the stuffed vegetables on a baking tray, pour over 2 tablespoons of vegetable oil to coat each piece evenly. Then sit them on the tray, ensuring none of the filling touches the tray itself, as it will stick. Roast for 20 minutes until the filling has become lightly browned and the prawn is coral pink in colour.

6
About 5 minutes before serving, heat 1 tablespoon of vegetable oil in a saucepan or wok over a medium heat. Add the ginger for the sauce and stir-fry for 30 seconds until fragrant. Then add the sauce, bring to the boil and continue boiling for 3–5 minutes, or until reduced by half. Pour over the stuffed vegetables, scatter over some chopped coriander to garnish and serve.

TIP This seafood mixture works really well as a stuffing for other vegetables, such as courgettes or marrows, or even large chillies (just be sure to take the seeds out before stuffing unless you like things ferociously hot!).

CANTONESE ROAST DUCK LEGS

SERVES 2

PREP 15 minutes, plus marinating
COOK 45 minutes

I once had a customer who really tested my knowledge. It seemed he cooked Chinese food at home more times in a week than I did, yet he still wanted to come for lessons. He was such an enthusiast, he even went as far as hanging a whole duck in his airing cupboard overnight, in with the clean bath towels and all. Needless to say his wife was not so enthusiastic! This recipe, a simplified version of the classic Cantonese roast duck and rice, is a great way to try something new – without ruining your clothes, towels or marriage...

2 duck legs
steamed jasmine rice, to serve

MARINADE

1 thumb-sized piece of ginger, peeled and finely sliced
1 spring onion, finely sliced
4 tablespoons honey
4 tablespoons red rice vinegar (swapsies: red wine vinegar)
2 tablespoons Shaoxing rice wine (swapsies: dry sherry)
1 tablespoon oyster sauce
½ tablespoon hoisin sauce
½ teaspoon Chinese five spice

1
Mix the marinade ingredients together in a mixing bowl.

2
Bring a saucepan of water to the boil, add the duck legs and blanch for 3 minutes. Remove from the pan and cool under cold running water, then drain and add the duck to the marinade. Using your hands, massage the marinade into the duck pieces until evenly coated. Cover and leave to marinate in the fridge overnight.

3
Preheat the oven to 160°C/350°F/Gas Mark 4.

4
Scoop the ginger and spring onion pieces up from the marinade (reserving the liquid in the bowl) and place on a roasting tray. Put the duck legs on top. Roast for 40 minutes, basting the legs with the reserved marinade every 10 minutes with a brush, until the skin is nicely caramelized.

5
Using a large, sharp knife or chopper, cut the duck legs into 2cm (¾ inch) thick pieces through the bone (see Tip). Arrange on top of a bed of steamed jasmine rice and serve with some Glazed Chinese Greens with Oyster Sauce (see page 202).

TIP When chopping through the bones of the duck legs, slice through the meat first, until you hit the bone. Now give the top of your knife or chopper a good hit with either your palm or a rolling pin to cut through the bone cleanly. This way you don't have to apply too much pressure with your bare hands and you won't end up hacking away at the meat.

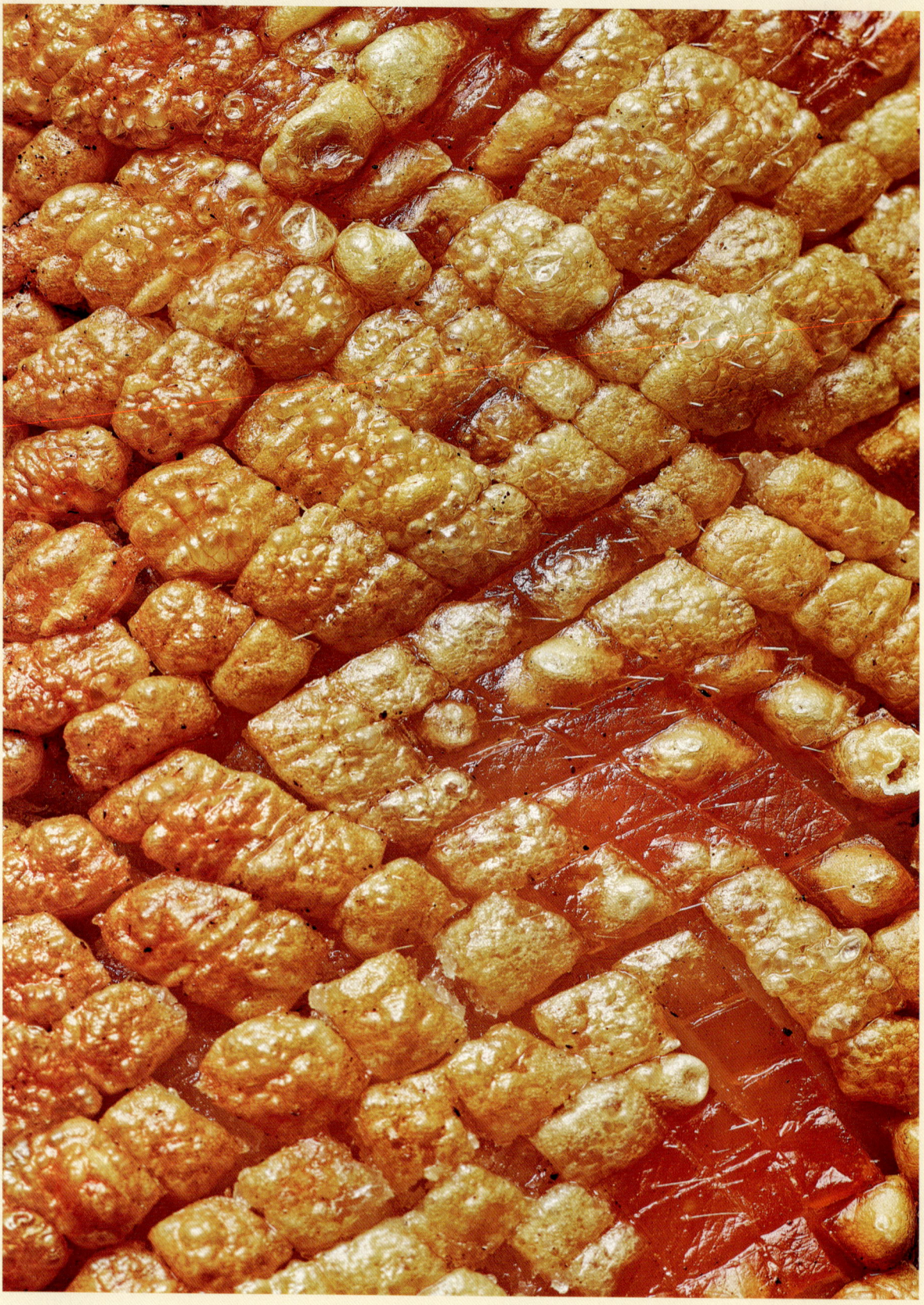

CRISPY PORK BELLY

PREP
15 minutes, plus resting

COOK
2¼–2½ hours

500g (1lb 2oz) pork belly, with skin
2 teaspoons salt
1–2 teaspoons Chinese five spice

SERVES 4

If there's one dish that brings together my extended family, it's crispy pork. A celebration doesn't feel right without it – so much so that a roast pig has made an appearance at the last two consecutive Pang weddings. In the final few days of my father's life he could barely even string a sentence together, yet he still managed to request a meal of crispy pork and rice, and smiled at the thought of it. And so this book would not be complete without it. The blanching process and initial slow cooking here will help to get rid of the many solid impurities and excess fat that pork seems to hold in its skin, while also softening the meat.

1

Place the pork belly piece, skin-side down, in a large saucepan and cover with boiling water. Bring to the boil, then reduce to a simmer and cook for 5 minutes before removing the meat from the pan. (Some scum may form on the top of the water, which is just some of the impurities and excess fat from the skin and will be discarded once the pork is blanched.)

2

Remove the meat from the pan and cool under cold running water. Drain and pat the skin dry with kitchen paper, then score gently using the tip of a sharp knife in diagonal criss-cross cuts along the top, trying to only open up the fat and not cut into the meat itself.

3

Dry the skin with kitchen paper once more and rub the salt into it. Rub the five spice onto the sides and bottom of the meat only, not the skin.

4

Preheat the oven to 130°C/300°F/Gas Mark 2. Place the pork, skin-side up, on a wire rack set over a roasting tray and roast in the oven for 1½ hours. Now turn the oven up to 230°C/500°F/Gas Mark 10 (or as high as your oven will go if it doesn't go this high) and roast for another 30–45 minutes, or until the skin is golden brown and crispy all the way through. To judge whether the pork skin is crispy enough, give it a flick with your finger: if the sound is hollow like that from the bottom of a well-baked loaf of bread, then the pork is definitely crispy enough.

5

Remove the pork from the oven and allow to rest for 15 minutes. Turn the pork, skin-side down, onto a chopping board and slice through the skin with a large sharp knife or cleaver, pressing down on the top of the blade to chop through the crackling, then serve.

TIP If you don't have a fan function on your oven, leave the pork out to dry in a cool, dry area of your kitchen for 1 hour before placing it in the oven.

SIZZLING PEPPER BEEF

SERVES 4

Here's a dish that takes me back to the eighties, but which seems to have kept its sizzle on Chinese restaurant menus and griddles around the world. I've swapped out the traditional stir-fry steaks for a more succulent, melt-in-the-mouth poached beef short rib, which takes the dish to the next level. If you have a pressure cooker or high-pressure steam oven, you could even cook the short rib in big batches and have it cooled, sliced and ready to finish off in no time for your own restaurant-quality meal!

PREP
15 minutes, plus cooling

COOK
3¼ hours

- 4 beef short ribs, separated
- ½ tablespoon sesame oil
- ½ red onion, sliced
- ½ green pepper, cored and sliced
- 2 large green chillies, roughly chopped
- 3–4 sticks of fresh green peppercorns

POACHING LIQUID

- 2 tablespoons loose jasmine tea
- 1 star anise
- 1 small cinnamon stick
- 2 cloves
- 2 bay leaves
- 1 tablespoon black peppercorns
- ½ teaspoon salt
- 1 litre water

SAUCE

- 1½ tablespoons freshly ground black pepper
- 1½ tablespoons oyster sauce
- 1 tablespoon light soy sauce
- 2 tablespoons Shaoxing rice wine
- 1 teaspoon sugar
- 100ml (3½fl oz) chicken stock
- 100ml (3½fl oz) lager (optional)

1
Place the short ribs into a large saucepan and add in the poaching liquid ingredients. Bring the pan to the boil over a high heat then, once boiling, lower the heat to a gentle simmer. Continue to poach the beef ribs over a low heat for 3 hours, until the meat starts to fall off the bone but still keeps its shape. Alternatively, place in a pressure cooker for 30 minutes.

2
Mix the sauce ingredients together in a large mixing bowl.

3
Once the ribs are poached, remove them from the poaching liquid. Discard the poaching liquid and allow the ribs to cool on a wire rack. Once cooled, slice the meat into 5-mm (¼-inch)-thick slices, cover with the sesame oil and set aside.

4
Build your wok clock. Start at 12 o'clock with the poached ribs, followed by the onion, pepper, green chillies and green peppercorns, and finally the sauce.

5
Heat a griddle pan to smoking point and lay each slice of beef onto the griddle. Sear well until charred on one side, then turn each piece to char the other side. Add the onion, green pepper and green peppercorns and sear until charred. Lastly, pour the sauce over the beef and allow to sizzle up for 1-2 minutes, then serve.

PREP
20 minutes

COOK
1 hour

500g (1lb 2oz) squid, cleaned and quills removed (ask the fishmonger to do this for you), tentacles separated and bodies kept whole

½ tablespoon cornflour

3 garlic cloves, finely chopped

1 small knob of ginger, peeled and finely chopped

1 teaspoon preserved fermented black beans, rinsed in cold water and drained

pinch of salt

1 red onion, cut into 1cm (½ inch) dice

3 spring onions, cut into rough chunks, plus extra, sliced, to garnish

2 large green chillies, cut into 1cm (½ inch) dice

vegetable oil

SAUCE

2 tablespoons oyster sauce

2 tablespoons Shaoxing rice wine (swapsies: dry sherry)

½ tablespoon light soy sauce

1 teaspoon sesame oil

½ teaspoon sugar

TWICE-COOKED SQUID WITH GARLIC & GREEN CHILLI

SERVES 4

In many parts of China and Hong Kong, cuttlefish are actually more popular than squid, and because they have much thicker meat than squid, the double-cooking process detailed here is essential. I find that large squid also benefit from this pre-poaching – it softens the seafood significantly, allowing the pieces to take in more flavour when stir-fried in the savoury sauce.

1

Slice the squid bodies open to lay them flat. Run the tip of your knife along the squid pieces in a diagonal criss-cross pattern (this will help the squid curl up nicely when cooking).

Bring a saucepan of water to the boil and add the prepared squid, then reduce the heat to a simmer and cook over a low heat for 45 minutes. Remove the squid from the water with a slotted spoon and cool under cold running water, then drain. Put the squid into a mixing bowl with the cornflour and mix together well.

2

Put the garlic and ginger into a small bowl with the black beans and salt, then lightly crush together with the back of a teaspoon.

Mix the sauce ingredients together in a small bowl.

3

Start at 12 o'clock with the red onion, followed by the spring onions, garlic, ginger and black bean mixture, green chillies, squid and finally the sauce.

4

Heat 1 tablespoon of vegetable oil in a wok over a high heat until smoking hot. Add the red onion and cook for 1 minute until slightly softened. Then add the spring onions and the garlic, ginger and black bean mixture and stir-fry for 30 seconds. Add the green chillies and stir-fry for 30 seconds, keeping the heat high all the time. Transfer the vegetable mixture to a bowl.

5

Add another ½ tablespoon of vegetable oil to the wok and heat to smoking point over a high heat. Add the squid and flash-fry for 30 seconds to sear it all over. Return the vegetable mixture to the wok, pour over the sauce and bring to a vigorous boil. Cook for 1–2 minutes until the sauce has reduced and thickened slightly and is just coating the squid and vegetables. Serve garnished with sliced spring onion.

PREP
15 minutes, plus drying & marinating

COOK
1¾–2¼ hours

NORTHERN CHINESE ROAST LAMB RIBS

SERVES 6–8

Much like many cuts of meat in Chinese cuisine, barbecued lamb ribs or ribs of any kind are often much chunkier and more meaty than the cut of ribs you might get in a Western supermarket. To make this as tasty as you might find in the northern parts of China, get to your local butcher and order some lamb ribs with a good bit of belly still attached and you'll be in for a treat.

1–1.5kg (2lb 4oz–3lb 5oz) lamb ribs, with as much lamb belly meat left on as possible

vegetable oil

POACHING LIQUID

3 spring onions, roughly chopped

1 leek, trimmed, cleaned and roughly chopped

1 thumb-sized piece of ginger, peeled and sliced

8 dried red chillies

1 tablespoon Sichuan peppercorns

2 litres (3½ pints) chicken stock

RUB

6 teaspoons cumin seeds

2 teaspoons fennel seeds

1 tablespoon sesame seeds

2 teaspoons chilli powder

1½ teaspoons salt

1 teaspoon coarsely ground black pepper

½ teaspoon sugar

1

Build your wok clock. Start at 12 o'clock with the lamb ribs, followed by the poaching liquid ingredients, cumin, fennel and sesame seeds for the rub and finally the rest of the rub ingredients.

2

Put the lamb ribs into a large saucepan, pour boiling water over to cover and bring to the boil, then reduce the heat and simmer the ribs for 5 minutes to get rid of any excess fatty impurities. Strain through a colander and rinse under cold running water.

3

Put all the poaching liquid ingredients into the pan and bring to a rolling boil. Add the lamb ribs and reduce to a simmer. Cover the pan with a lid and poach the ribs for 1½–2 hours until tender.

4

Meanwhile, for the rub, toast the cumin, fennel and sesame seeds in a dry frying pan over a medium heat for 1–2 minutes, swirling every 30 seconds to make sure they don't burn. Remove them from the pan and allow to cool, then grind to a coarse powder with the rest of the rub ingredients using a pestle and mortar or spice grinder. Set aside.

5

Once the ribs have finished poaching, remove them from the poaching liquid with a slotted spoon and place them on a wire rack. Pat each rib dry with kitchen paper and allow to dry out for at least 1 hour.

6

Rub about 1 teaspoon of vegetable oil over each lamb rib and then rub at least 1–2 teaspoons of the rub all over the ribs. Cover and leave to marinate in the fridge for at least 1 hour, preferably overnight.

7

Preheat the oven on the grill function to at least 230°C/450°F, but ideally 250°C/480°F. Grill the ribs for 4–5 minutes on each side until the fat is crispy all over. Serve immediately with any excess rub on the side to dip in for more flavour.

PREP
10 minutes

COOK
10 minutes

500g (1lb 2oz) fine green beans, trimmed

1 onion, finely sliced

1 large knob of ginger, peeled and finely sliced

4 garlic cloves, peeled and sliced

2 birds' eye chillies, diced

vegetable oil

SAUCE

2 tablespoons hoisin sauce

2 tablespoons Shaoxing rice wine (swapsies: dry sherry)

2 teaspoons Chiu Chow chilli oil

a generous dash of dark soy sauce

1 tablespoon light soy sauce

DOUBLE-COOKED GREEN BEANS WITH CHILLI HOISIN

SERVES 4 AS A MAIN OR 8 AS A SIDE

The double-cooking process here for the beans may seem like a lot of effort, but it will leave them soft and succulent and is well worth it. The traditional way to cook this dish is to deep-fry the beans first before flash-frying and then tossing them into the slightly sweet, slightly spicy sauce. However, on the home front, I find it a bit too much to use a whole litre (1¾ pints) of oil just for a bag of beans, and I do think the dish comes out just as well by blanching them in hot water rather than hot oil.

1

Bring a saucepan of water to the boil, add the beans and blanch for 2 minutes. Drain and cool under cold running water, then drain well again.

Mix the sauce ingredients together in a small bowl or ramekin.

2

Build your wok clock. Start at 12 o'clock with the onion, followed by the ginger and garlic, blanched green beans and finally the birds' eye chillies and sauce.

3

Heat 1½ tablespoons of vegetable oil in a wok over a high heat until smoking hot. Add the onion and stir-fry for 1 minute until slightly softened, then add the ginger and garlic and stir-fry for 30 seconds.

4

Keeping the heat as high as possible, add the blanched green beans and stir-fry for 2–3 minutes until they have blistered around the edges. Then add the chillies and sauce, bring to a vigorous boil and continue to cook, stirring, for 2–3 minutes until the sauce has reduced and is just coating the beans. Remove from the heat, spoon into a large serving bowl and serve.

TIP The spiciness of the green beans balances very well with something delicate like the Steamed Fish with Ginger & Spring Onions (see page 130). Add a bowl of steamed jasmine rice to make a lovely simple dinner for 3 or 4 people.

TWICE-COOKED CHILLI PORK

PREP 20 minutes, plus drying & marinating

COOK 1–2¼ hours

SERVES 4

This succulent yet crisp pork belly is a great recipe for a special occasion – just poach and cool the meat on the day before you want to serve it, leaving you very little to do on the day itself. The flavours added to the poaching liquid bring a subtle depth of flavour to the stir-fry, while the initial poaching softens the meat well, giving a unique texture and bite to the dish.

300g (10½oz) pork belly, with skin
2 star anise
1 cinnamon stick
2 cloves
5 black peppercorns
1 onion, cut into thin strips
1 small knob of ginger, peeled and finely sliced
2 garlic cloves, finely sliced
2 large red chillies, diced
vegetable oil
small handful of coriander, roughly chopped, to garnish

MARINADE

2 teaspoons cornflour
2 teaspoons sesame oil
¼ teaspoon salt
¼ teaspoon black pepper

SAUCE

½ tablespoon hoisin sauce
½ tablespoon Shaoxing rice wine (swapsies: dry sherry)
½ tablespoon Chinkiang vinegar (swapsies: rice vinegar)
1 teaspoon chilli bean sauce (*toban jiang*)
1 teaspoon chilli oil
dash of dark soy sauce

1

Put the pork belly into a saucepan with the star anise, cinnamon, cloves and black peppercorns. Cover with hot water, bring to a simmer and poach for at least 45 minutes, preferably up to 2 hours. Remove the meat from the pan, discard the poaching liquid, and cool the pork under cold running water. Drain and pat the skin dry with kitchen paper, then place the pork on a plate, cover and leave to chill in the fridge for at least 1 hour, preferably overnight.

When you are ready to cook, remove the pork from the fridge and thinly slice. Put the slices into a mixing bowl, add the marinade ingredients and massage them into the meat slices until evenly coated. Then cover and leave to marinate for 20 minutes.

Mix the sauce ingredients together in a small bowl or ramekin.

2

Build your wok clock. Start at 12 o'clock with the onion, followed by the ginger, garlic and red chillies, marinated poached pork and finally the sauce.

3

Heat 1 tablespoon of vegetable oil in a wok over a high heat until smoking. Add the onion and stir-fry for 1 minute until slightly softened, then add the ginger, garlic and chillies and stir-fry for 1 minute until fragrant and smoky.

4

Push the vegetables to the back of the wok, add another tablespoon of vegetable oil and heat to smoking point. Then add the pork slices, spread them out in a single layer and leave to sear for 1 minute until browned. Turn the pork slices over and sear on the other side.

5

Spoon the other ingredients over the top of the pork and pour over the sauce. Bring to a vigorous boil and cook, stirring, for 2–3 minutes until the sauce has thickened and coats the meat nicely. Spoon onto a serving plate, scatter over the coriander to garnish and serve.

TIP The long cooling period after poaching will help to tighten the meat up and allow any soft fats to solidify once again, making it much easier to slice the next day.

PREP
10 minutes

COOK
2–3½ hours

30 spare ribs
4 garlic cloves, finely chopped
1 large knob of ginger, peeled and finely chopped
8 tablespoons tomato ketchup
8 tablespoons hoisin sauce
4 tablespoons sugar
4 tablespoons dark soy sauce
4 tablespoons rice vinegar
2 tablespoons vegetable oil
500ml–1 litre (18fl oz–1¾ pints) cola or cider
½ spring onion, finely chopped, to garnish

BARBECUED HOISIN & COLA RIBS

SERVES 6–8

These delicious little nuggets never fail to bring in a crowd. They are sweet, sticky and tender, cheap to make and simple to prepare, yet guaranteed to be a showstopper at any dinner party or barbecue. They do, however, require a long, slow cook – 2–3 hours ideally – to ensure the meat is succulent and falling off the bone, so make sure you plan ahead.

1

Preheat the oven to 150°C/340°F/Gas Mark 3½.

2

Put the ribs into a deep roasting tray or large ovenproof pot along with all the other ingredients except the spring onion. Mix everything together thoroughly, ensuring the ribs are well covered.

3

Cook in the oven, uncovered, for at least 2–3 hours, basting and turning the ribs every so often to prevent them from burning (if they do start to catch, turn the oven down slightly). Towards the end of the cooking time, the ribs will start to break up and fall apart slightly – this is a good sign, but you want to keep them as whole as possible (ready for grilling), so be careful when turning.

4

Switch the oven onto the grill function and preheat to 230°C/450°F. Remove the ribs from the oven, reserving any extra sauce from the roasting tray, and grill, in batches, for 2–3 minutes on each side until the outsides of the ribs are glazed and charred. Drizzle over a little of the remaining sauce, sprinkle over the spring onion to garnish and serve. (Although the ribs are always better after they have been grilled slightly, if you just can't wait, they can always be eaten straight after roasting in the oven.)

TIP The final stage of cooking can also be done on a hot outdoor barbecue if the weather allows.

PREP
10 minutes

COOK
40 minutes

300g (10½oz) chicken wings

¼ teaspoon Chinese five spice

1 thumb-sized piece of ginger, peeled and cut into fine matchsticks

1 garlic clove, finely diced

1 large red chilli, finely diced

about 300ml (10fl oz) water

vegetable oil

SAUCE

4 tablespoons plum sauce

1 teaspoon chilli bean sauce (*toban jiang*)

dash of dark soy sauce

CHILLI & PLUM SAUCE WINGS

SERVES 4

Certain meats like chicken wings or pork belly are quite difficult to cook quickly from raw on a grill or barbecue, as the fatty skin tends to catch and burn much sooner than the meat itself takes to cook. Braising the chicken wings first helps to break down the waxiness of the skin and packs the flavour of the braising liquid into the meat, while cooking it through thoroughly. Cooking your chicken wings this way gives them a perfect chargrilled finish that makes them irresistibly moreish.

1
Mix the sauce ingredients together in a small bowl or ramekin.

2
Build your wok clock. Start at 12 o'clock with the chicken wings, followed by the five spice, ginger, garlic and red chilli, sauce and finally the measured hot water.

3
Heat 1 tablespoon of vegetable oil in a saucepan over a medium heat. Add the chicken wings and cook, turning, for 2–3 minutes until browned on all sides.

4
Add the five spice, ginger, garlic and chilli and cook, stirring, for 1 minute. Then pour over the sauce, bring to the boil and continue boiling for 3–5 minutes, stirring continuously, until it reduces and coats the chicken wings. Add enough of the measured hot water just to cover the chicken wings and bring to a simmer. Cover the pan with a lid and simmer for 15–20 minutes over a low heat until the chicken is cooked through but the skin is still intact.

5
Transfer the wings to a roasting tray with a slotted spoon, reserving the sauce for basting.

6
Finish the wings off in the oven on the grill function preheated to 230°C/450°F for 3–5 minutes, or on a hot barbecue. Baste with the excess sauce every minute or so, until the wings are lightly charred and caramelized. Serve immediately.

CRISPY DUCK BREAST WITH PANCAKES & CUCUMBER PICKLE

SERVES 4

PREP 30 minutes
COOK 30 minutes

2 large duck breasts
½ teaspoon salt
¼ teaspoon Chinese five spice
16–20 duck pancakes
3 tablespoons hoisin sauce (optional)

CUCUMBER PICKLE

½ cucumber, cut into fine matchsticks
1 spring onion, cut into fine matchsticks
1 garlic clove, finely sliced
8 Sichuan peppercorns, crushed using a pestle and mortar
2 tablespoons sugar
2 tablespoons Chinkiang vinegar (swapsies: rice vinegar)
1 tablespoon hot water
½ tablespoon light soy sauce
¼ teaspoon salt

DIPPING SAUCE

2 tablespoons cold water
4 teaspoons plum sauce
2 teaspoons chilli garlic sauce
dash of dark soy sauce

Here is my simple take on a duck and pancake recipe that brings together double-cooking and roasting techniques from both Chinese and Western backgrounds. I like the duck breast medium-rare, but the skin should be as crispy as possible; the initial blanching dissolves the skin's outer layer so it becomes crispier when fried and roasted. The plum dipping sauce is a fresh alternative to the classic hoisin, but for any purists at the table, why not have both?

1

Mix the ingredients for the cucumber pickle together well in a small bowl.

Mix the dipping sauce ingredients together in a separate small bowl or ramekin.

2

Put the duck breasts into a saucepan and cover with boiling water. Bring back to the boil and blanch for 2–3 minutes. Remove the duck from the pan and cool under cold running water. Drain and pat the skin dry with kitchen paper, then score gently using the tip of a sharp knife in diagonal cuts along the top, trying only to open up the fat and not cut into the meat itself.

3

Rub the salt into the duck breasts and then dab the skin dry with kitchen paper. Rub the five spice onto the sides and bottom of the meat only, not the skin. Dab the skin dry once more to remove any extra moisture.

4

Preheat the oven to 200°C/425°F/Gas Mark 7.

5

Place the duck breasts, skin-side down, in a cold frying pan and let the pan heat up to a medium-high heat. Fry for 6–8 minutes, or until the skin is golden brown, pressing down on the sides to ensure all parts of the skin become crispy.

6

Place the duck breasts, skin-side up, on a wire rack set over a roasting tray and roast in the oven for 6–8 minutes to your liking. Remove the duck from the oven and leave to rest for 5 minutes.

7

While the duck breast is resting, line a bamboo steamer basket with a silicon steam mat or greased baking paper. Put the pancakes inside the basket, cover with the lid and place over a wok a third filled with boiling water. Steam for 3–5 minutes.

8

Cut the duck into thin slices and serve with the pickle, dipping sauce and hoisin sauce (if using) accompanied by the pancakes in the steamer.

PREP
20 minutes

COOK
10 minutes

SUPER-CRISPY TWICE-FRIED PRAWNS IN SWEET SOY

SERVES 4

Cooking a dish like this perfectly is a little step up from just deep-frying some prawns and throwing a sauce on top. The deep-fry at the beginning of this double-cooking process acts as a gentle blanch in hot oil that seals the prawns lightly, allowing the sauce to seep through the air pockets within the meat and shells, leaving a sensational flavour on your palate.

500g (1lb 2oz) shell-on large raw tiger prawns

2 tablespoons cornflour

½ red onion, finely sliced

1 thumb-sized piece of ginger, peeled and cut into matchsticks

1 medium tomato, cut into wedges

vegetable oil, for deep-frying

sea salt and black pepper

large handful of coriander, roughly chopped, to garnish

SAUCE

100ml (3½fl oz) chicken or fish stock

2 tablespoons dark soy sauce

1 tablespoon rice vinegar

1 tablespoon sugar

1

Mix the sauce ingredients together in a small bowl or ramekin.

To devein the prawns while keeping them intact, insert a cocktail stick roughly three-quarters of the way up the back of the prawn and pull the dark vein up and out of the shell. Put the prawns into a mixing bowl, add the cornflour and season with salt and black pepper. Then, using your hands, massage the cornflour into the prawns until evenly coated.

2

Build your wok clock. Start at 12 o'clock with the coated prawns, followed by the red onion, ginger, tomato and finally the sauce.

3

Half-fill a wok with vegetable oil and heat to 160°C/325°F, or until the tip of a wooden chopstick or skewer starts to bubble (but not fizz) after 2–3 seconds in the oil. Carefully add the prawns to the hot oil and deep-fry for 2 minutes until they are a pale coral colour and the shells are slightly browned. Set a sieve over a saucepan and carefully transfer the prawns from the oil into the sieve. Then pour the oil over the prawns for an extra sizzle and to remove the oil from the wok.

4

Heat 1 tablespoon of vegetable oil in the wok over a high heat until smoking hot. Add the red onion and stir-fry for 30 seconds, then add the ginger and then the tomato, stir-frying for 30 seconds after each addition.

5

Keeping the heat as high as possible, pour the sauce into the wok and bring to a vigorous boil. Add the prawns and cook for 1–2 minutes until the sauce has thickened and forms a coating around them. Transfer to a serving dish, scatter over the coriander to garnish and serve.

BEIJING GRIDDLED BEEF

PREP
15 minutes, plus marinating

COOK
15 minutes

SERVES 4

There is an art to this type of old school Chinese barbecuing, chefs usually cook this at your table with cooking chopsticks poised, ready to turn each piece of meat at the right moment to ensure it is cooked perfectly. The meat should be seared to get a little colour, but the desired texture of the meat, cooked to medium, is what's important. The spring onion base acts as a protective layer between the griddle and the beef, and also adds a unique, savoury flavour to the dish.

600g (1lb 5oz) beef rump steak, finely sliced and flattened with the side of the cleaver (see page 20)

8 spring onions, diagonally sliced into 3–4cm (1¼–1½ inch) lengths

vegetable oil

large handful of coriander, leaves picked, stalks roughly chopped

3 egg yolks

5–6 leaves of sweetheart cabbage, finely shredded

MARINADE

2 thumb-sized pieces of ginger, peeled and roughly chopped

6 tablespoons light soy sauce

4 tablespoons Shaoxing rice wine (swapsies: dry sherry)

4 teaspoons sesame oil

4 teaspoons sugar

1

Blitz the marinade ingredients together in a food processor to a smooth paste. If you don't have a food processor, just finely chop the ginger and mix with the rest of the marinade ingredients.

Put the beef into a mixing bowl, add the marinade and, using your hands, massage it into the meat strips until evenly coated. Cover and leave to marinate in the fridge for at least 1 hour, preferably overnight.

2

Put the spring onions into a mixing bowl with 1 tablespoon of vegetable oil and toss the oil through the spring onions.

3

Build your wok clock. Start at 12 o'clock with the oiled spring onions, followed by the marinated beef, coriander stalks and leaves, the egg yolks and finally the shredded cabbage.

4

Heat a griddle pan over a high heat until smoking hot. Place the spring onions on the hot griddle and stir-fry for 2–3 minutes until they begin to wilt and brown slightly. Start to add the beef on top of the spring onions, keeping any remaining marinade aside in the bowl. Once all the beef has been laid on top of the spring onions, mix the spring onions in with the beef to prevent them from overcooking or burning and to allow the beef to sear slightly on the hot griddle. Then fold in the coriander stalks and picked leaves.

5

Once the beef is cooked to medium, after about 1–2 minutes, pour any remaining marinade over the top. Create a small hollow in the centre of the pile of beef, add the egg yolks and stir it into the hot beef just before serving.

6

Serve the beef, then add the shredded cabbage to the hot griddle to mop up the sauce and serve alongside.

TIP This dish is best enjoyed when the griddle pan can be placed on a barbecue or cooked at the table using a portable gas stove.

CHAPTER 6
SALADS, PICKLES & SIDES

SALADS, PICKLES & SIDES

AS I MENTIONED at the very beginning of this book, trying to find the right balance in flavour, texture and colour is, for me, one of the most important things to learn about cooking and eating Chinese food. No good Chinese meal, no matter how delicious, rich or flavourful, is complete without a side vegetable or pickle to balance out the concentrated flavours of the deep-fried meats, slippery noodles and stir-fried rich seafood.

Pickling has been a significant form of food preservation all over China since pre-refrigeration days, as it has been across many cultures. Though no longer essential, it still deserves its place at the dinner table as well as here in this book. Over the next few pages you will find some simple pickles to go on the side of any meal you decide to cook from this book, all of which can be eaten after just 45–60 minutes of pickling, if not straight away.

COOKING TIMES FOR CHINESE GREENS

The quick vegetable sides dishes here will also provide a fresh finish to any meal. When ordering at a Chinese restaurant, or planning meals at home, the last thing I usually tend to order or plan are the Chinese greens. Usually the restaurant server will have a list of the kitchen's seasonal greens ready to reel off to you; at home I'll just duck my head into the fridge to see what's lying around. Serve these with your main course and some steamed rice and you will feel like you are eating in a family home in Hong Kong or China in no time!

The most important thing to note when cooking your vegetables is to try not to overcook them. Below is a general guide for cooking the most commonly found Chinese greens, whether you are stir-frying, blanching, or steaming them.

TUNG CHOI (MORNING GLORY)

stir-fry, blanch or steam for 1–2 minutes

KAI CHOI (CHINESE MUSTARD GREENS)

stir-fry, blanch or steam for 2 minutes

PAK CHOI

stir-fry, blanch or steam for 3 minutes

CHOI SUM

stir-fry, blanch or steam for 4 minutes

KAI LAN (CHINESE BROCCOLI)

stir-fry, blanch or steam for 5 minutes

PREP
10 minutes

COOK
2 minutes

250g (9oz) morning glory (*tung choi*)
3 garlic cloves, unpeeled
2 birds' eye chillies
1 thumb-sized piece of ginger, peeled and finely sliced
1 tablespoon Shaoxing rice wine (swapsies: dry sherry)
1 tablespoon oyster sauce
½ tablespoon light soy sauce
1 teaspoon sesame oil
vegetable oil

FLASH-FRIED MORNING GLORY

SERVES 2

While visiting Thailand a few years ago I suffered serious wok envy. My wife and I had been commissioned to write a travel book in Phuket and had stumbled across a market in the old town offering all types of mouth-watering Chinese and Thai street treats. There was one old Chinese man cooking by a fierce wok burner who stood out from the rest – you could barely see what he was doing through the flames, but his wok work was absolutely mesmerizing. We ordered a plate of the vegetables, and it was amazing how he made something so simple taste so good.

1

Chop the morning glory stalks into about 5cm (2 inch) lengths and put them into a large mixing bowl along with all the leaves.

2

Using the flat side of a knife or cleaver, smash the garlic cloves to release their flavour and remove the skins. Pierce the chillies several times with the tip of a sharp knife, being sure to keep them whole and the stems intact (this will release a bit of the chilli heat and flavour, without making everything overwhelmingly spicy).

3

Add the garlic, chillies and ginger to the bowl along with the rice wine, sauces and sesame oil and mix together well.

4

Heat 2 tablespoons of vegetable oil in a wok over a high heat until smoking hot. Add the vegetable mixture and stir-fry for 1–2 minutes until the morning glory is tender but still retains its shape and vibrant colour. Serve immediately.

TIP Be careful not to overcook this dish! So long as it is piping hot and has a good glaze to its outer stem, the morning glory is ready to eat. The whole stalk and all the leaves are edible, so be sure to use every part of the morning glory when flash-frying.

PREP
5 minutes

COOK
2 minutes

2 garlic cloves, finely chopped

vegetable oil

2 handfuls of pea shoots, rinsed and well drained

SAUCE

100ml (3½fl oz) chicken or vegetable stock

1 tablespoon Shaoxing rice wine (swapsies: dry sherry)

1 teaspoon sesame oil

¼ teaspoon salt

STIR-FRIED PEA SHOOTS WITH GARLIC

SERVES 2

When you order in a Cantonese restaurant, if you are speaking to the waiters in Chinese, the first thing they will ask is what type of tea you would like – reeling off a huge list so quickly that you most probably won't understand, even if you are Chinese yourself! After this, they will do the same for the types of fresh green vegetables that they have in that day, and once you have chosen, they will ask you, 'With garlic, or oyster sauce?' If they ever have pea shoots in, try them with garlic – they are best eaten this way and are one of my favourite vegetables.

1

Mix the sauce ingredients together in a jug or bowl.

2

Heat 1 tablespoon of vegetable oil in a wok over a high heat until smoking hot. Add the garlic, immediately followed by the pea shoots, and stir-fry for 30 seconds until the garlic is fragrant.

3

Pour the sauce into the wok, bring to a vigorous boil and cook for 1 minute until the pea shoots have wilted but are still vibrant in colour. Serve immediately.

TIP If your sauce is not thick enough after boiling, mix 2 teaspoons of cornflour with 2 tablespoons of cold water, stir the mixture into the sauce and cook until thickened before serving.

PREP
5 minutes

COOK
5 minutes

300–400g (10½–14oz) Chinese greens (such as pak choi, choi sum or Chinese broccoli (*kai lin*)

vegetable oil

1 tablespoon oyster sauce, to serve

GLAZED CHINESE GREENS WITH OYSTER SAUCE

SERVES 2

The Chinese don't like to overcook or overpower their greens, as they really are the balancing act to what could otherwise be a very meat-filled, seafood-heavy meal. Simply blanch your greens (whichever you choose) and follow the timings below to provide the perfect counter to a Chinese dish. Instead of using water, try boiling the vegetables in chicken or vegetable stock to add a little extra flavour.

1

Bring a large saucepan or wok of water to a rapid boil. Add the vegetables and boil for 1–5 minutes until tender (see pages 196–7 for specific vegetable cooking times).

2

Drain and place on a large serving plate. Using a pair of sharp scissors, cut the vegetables into bite-sized pieces (see Tip).

3

Heat ½ a tablespoon of vegetable oil in a small saucepan or wok until smoking hot, then remove from the heat and pour over the top of the greens. Serve piping hot with the oyster sauce on the side.

TIP To add a bit of style to the presentation of this simple dish, I like to employ a trick that is used in Chinese restaurants: line up your whole-cooked vegetables neatly on a serving plate, then run a pair of scissors through them and cut them into bite-sized chunks, while trying to keep the vegetables aligned so that they still look whole. This makes the dish more interesting visually as well as making it easier to eat.

PICKLED CARROT & DAIKON

PREP
20 minutes,
plus pickling

1 carrot, cut into fine matchsticks

½ daikon, peeled and cut into fine matchsticks (swapsies: 300g/ 10½oz any radish)

PICKLING LIQUID

250ml (9fl oz) warm water

3 tablespoons distilled vinegar or rice vinegar

3 tablespoons caster sugar

2 tablespoons salt

SERVES 4

No matter what type of pickle you are making, bear in mind that the idea is to have an intense hit of sour, sweet and salty in every bite. The next tip is to use vegetables that have both a good bite and absorb flavour well – whether crunchy or fibrous. Here, the carrot and daikon provide excellent texture as well as a great contrast in colour, and are guaranteed to look appetizing on the side of any main dish.

1

Mix the pickling liquid ingredients together in a large mixing bowl until the sugar and salt have fully dissolved.

2

Fill a clean, tight-lidded jar or other lidded container with the carrot and daikon. Pour over the pickling liquid until the vegetables are fully covered and the container is full. Pop on the lid and leave to pickle for a minimum of 1 hour for immediate use, or up to 3 days for maximum flavour.

PREP
20 minutes, plus pickling

COOK
5 minutes

8–10cm (3¼–4 inch) lotus root segment (see Tip, page 132), peeled and cut into 2mm (¹⁄₁₆ inch) thick slices

100g (3½oz) Chinese spinach or baby spinach leaves

PICKLING LIQUID

150ml (5fl oz) Chinkiang vinegar (swapsies: rice vinegar)

100ml (3½fl oz) hot water

8 tablespoons caster sugar

4 tablespoons sesame oil

2 tablespoons salt

4 garlic cloves, finely sliced

20 Sichuan peppercorns, lightly crushed using a pestle and mortar

3 star anise

PICKLED LOTUS ROOT & SPINACH

SERVES 4

Lotus root is essentially a natural filter – its porous texture absorbs flavour and moisture, making it easy to pickle. The best thing about pickling lotus root is that it keeps its crunch and has an earthy taste, which holds and complements the flavour of the pickling liquid. Adding the spinach accentuates that earthiness, while its contrasting softness brings out the lotus root's great texture.

1
Mix the pickling liquid ingredients together in a mixing bowl until the sugar has fully dissolved.

2
Bring a saucepan of water to the boil, add the lotus root slices and blanch for 3 minutes. Remove from the pan and cool under cold running water, then drain.

3
Fill a clean, tight-lidded jar or lidded container with the blanched lotus root and spinach leaves and pour over the pickling liquid until the vegetables are fully covered and the container is full. Pop on the lid and leave to pickle for a minimum of 45 minutes for immediate use, or up to 1 day for maximum flavour.

TIP Lotus root tends to come in vacuum packs containing 3–4 root segments, which would probably be too much for just one recipe. To stop any going to waste, try making this recipe alongside the Five Spice Lotus Leaf Chicken with Chinese Sausage (see page 132).

PREP
20 minutes, plus soaking & pickling

COOK
5 minutes

250g (9oz) waxy potato (such as Désirée or new potatoes), peeled and cut into fine matchsticks

2 garlic cloves, finely chopped

1 spring onion, cut into fine matchsticks

4 dried red chillies, soaked in hot water for 15 minutes, then drained and roughly chopped

sea salt

PICKLING MIXTURE

4 tablespoons rice vinegar

2 tablespoon light soy sauce

2 teaspoons sugar

1 teaspoon sesame oil

PICKLED POTATO WITH CHILLI & GARLIC

SERVES 4

If you've ever had a leftover potato that just needs using up in your cupboard, this is one of the quickest and tastiest ways to eat it. It's as close to raw as you can possibly get, and most people would never in their wildest dreams eat a raw potato, but blanching thin slices of potato for a short space of time, cooks out the raw chalky texture while keeping all the goodness. And it's a great crunchy salad to use as a side for any meal.

1
Bring a saucepan of water to the boil, add the potato along with 1 teaspoon of sea salt and blanch for 1 minute. Remove from the pan and cool under cold running water, then drain.

2
Using a pestle and mortar or the flat side of a knife, grind the garlic with a pinch of sea salt into a paste.

3
Mix the pickling mixture ingredients together in a small bowl until the sugar has fully dissolved.

4
Pour the pickling mixture over the potato, spring onion, dried red chillies and garlic paste, and toss through until fully coated. Serve immediately. Alternatively, this will keep in a sealed airtight container in the fridge for up to 2 days, and it will take on more and more flavour the longer it sits.

TIP This fresh pickle is fantastic for adding a crunch to a bowl of blanched or steamed dumplings. If you fancy an alternative light lunch with bold Chinese flavours, try this dish with a portion of the Wontons in Chilli Broth (see page 124).

MUSTARD GREENS & PAK CHOI SALAD

SERVES 2

PREP
20 minutes, plus soaking

COOK
5 minutes

- 3 tablespoons sesame seeds
- ½ daikon, peeled and finely sliced
- 100g (3½oz) kai choi (Chinese mustard greens), roughly chopped
- 100g (3½oz) pak choi, roughly chopped
- 3 dried wood ear mushroom florets, soaked in hot water for at least 2 hours, preferably overnight, then drained and roughly chopped
- large handful of coriander, roughly chopped
- 3–4 radishes, finely sliced
- 50g (1¾oz) Pickled Carrot & Daikon (see page 203) (optional)

DRESSING

- 1 small knob of ginger, peeled and finely chopped
- 1 garlic clove, finely chopped
- 4 tablespoons freshly squeezed lime juice
- 1 tablespoon sesame paste (swapsies: tahini)
- 1 tablespoon sugar
- 1 tablespoon light soy sauce
- 2 teaspoons sesame oil
- pinch of salt

Although it is not necessarily typical to eat raw vegetables in most parts of China, some of our traditional greens hold a great deal of flavour and make great simple salads like this one. Kai choi and pak choi are both from the mustard family – when eaten raw, they have a slightly peppery and distinct mustardy flavour that goes very well with bittersweet radish and daikon. Adding the pickled veg to the salad gives the dish a nice extra variation of texture, but it is not essential if you are short on time.

1
Mix the dressing ingredients together in a small bowl until smooth.

2
Toast the sesame seeds in a dry wok over a medium heat for 2–3 minutes until fragrant and golden brown, then set aside.

3
Bring a saucepan of water to the boil, add the daikon and blanch for 1 minute. Remove the daikon from the pan and cool under cold running water, then drain.

4
Put all the salad ingredients except the sesame seeds into a mixing bowl, pour over the dressing and toss until evenly coated. Scatter over the toasted sesame seeds and serve.

PREP
20 minutes, plus soaking

COOK
15 minutes

- 100g (3½oz) dried mung bean vermicelli noodles
- 100g (3½oz) boneless, skinless chicken breast or thigh
- 1 tablespoon sesame seeds
- ½ carrot, cut into fine matchsticks
- ½ cucumber, cut into fine matchsticks
- 2 spring onions, cut into fine matchsticks

DRESSING

- 2 tablespoons chilli oil
- 2 tablespoons light soy sauce
- 1 tablespoon chicken stock
- 1 tablespoon sesame paste (swapsies: tahini)
- 1½ teaspoons Chinkiang vinegar (swapsies: rice vinegar)
- 1½ teaspoons sugar
- 1 teaspoon sesame oil
- ½ teaspoon Sichuan peppercorns, crushed

GLASS NOODLE CHICKEN SALAD

SERVES 4

Mung bean vermicelli are a type of glass noodle that become almost transparent when cooked. They bring a slightly jelly-like bite to a dish and make a great addition to salads and soups. Light, fresh and healthy-tasting, this is one salad I could happily eat for lunch every day, though it also works well as a dinner party side or as an accompaniment to a summer barbecue.

1
Soak the noodles in hot water for 5 minutes until they have softened but are still al dente. Drain and leave to dry on a clean tea towel until you are ready to use them.

2
Bring a saucepan of water to the boil, add the chicken and poach for 7–10 minutes, or until cooked through. Remove from the pan, drain and slice into thin shreds.

3
Toast the sesame seeds in a dry wok over a medium heat for 2–3 minutes until fragrant and golden brown, then set aside.

4
Mix the dressing ingredients together in a small bowl until the sugar has fully dissolved.

5
Put all the salad ingredients except the sesame seeds into a mixing bowl, pour over the dressing and toss until evenly coated. Transfer the dressed salad to a serving plate, scatter over the toasted sesame seeds and serve.

TIP Try varying this dish by switching the mung bean vermicelli for sweet potato, spinach or cassava noodles instead.

THREE SLIVER SALAD

SERVES 4

PREP
10 minutes, plus soaking & chilling

COOK
10 minutes

1 carrot, cut into thin strips

200g (7oz) tofu skin (swapsies: firm tofu), cut into thin strips

2 sheets of dried sea kelp, soaked in cold water for 15 minutes, then drained and cut into thin strips

DRESSING

1 garlic clove, finely chopped

small handful of coriander, stalks roughly chopped, leaves picked and reserved for the salad

1 teaspoon chilli flakes

2–3 tablespoons vegetable oil

3 tablespoons Chingkiang black vinegar (swapsies: rice vinegar)

1½ tablespoons light soy sauce

1 tablespoon sugar

This salad is all about adding texture and bite to your meal. The blanched seaweed and carrot both weave a lovely crunchy texture into the unique bite and chew of the tofu skin while the chilli oil dressing makes the salad jump out as a great accompaniment to sweeter braised dishes and a big bowl of steamed rice.

1

Fill a wok two-thirds full of hot water and bring to the boil over a high heat. Then fill a mixing bowl with ice-cold water for cooling the ingredients once they have been blanched.

2

Once the water is boiling, blanch the carrot for 30 seconds, remove it with a slotted spoon and then dunk into the cold water to cool and stop any further cooking. Remove the cooled carrot from the cold water and put it into a large mixing bowl.

3

Blanch the tofu skin for 2–3 minutes, then cool in the cold water and add to the carrot. Repeat the 2–3 minutes blanching and cooling process for the sea kelp and add it to the carrot and tofu.

4

Give the blanched ingredients a quick toss through and then place them in the fridge for at least 30 minutes to chill.

5

For the dressing, mix together the garlic, coriander stalks and chilli flakes in a small heatproof bowl. Heat the vegetable oil in a small pan or wok over a medium-high heat until smoking hot, then remove from the heat and wait for 10–20 seconds before pouring it over the garlic mixture to create a quick sizzle. Then add the rest of the dressing ingredients and mix well.

6

When ready to serve, pour the dressing over the salad, add the reserved coriander leaves and serve.

PREP
30 minutes, plus rising & resting

COOK
15 minutes

BEIJING SESAME BREAD

SERVES 4

This deliciously savoury bread (*zhi ma shao bing*), features a layer of spiced nuttiness inside and works a treat on the side of the Beijing Griddled Beef (see page 191), but for me it's a great side dish to mop up any saucy stir-fry or barbecued dish, or just to eat as a snack on its own with the dipping sauce.

200g (7oz) sesame seeds
vegetable oil

DOUGH

240g (8½oz) plain flour
5g (⅛oz) fast-action dried yeast
½ teaspoon sugar
120ml (4fl oz) warm water
2 teaspoons vegetable oil, plus extra for oiling

DIPPING SAUCE (OPTIONAL)

½ teaspoon sesame seeds
1 tablespoon hoisin sauce
1 tablespoon light soy sauce
½ tablespoon Worcestershire sauce
2 teaspoons Sichuan Pepper Chilli Oil (see page 41)
1 teaspoon Chiu Chow chilli oil

FILLING

1 teaspoon fennel seeds
¼ teaspoon Sichuan peppercorns
6 tablespoons sesame paste (swapsies: smooth peanut butter)
½ teaspoon salt
¼ teaspoon sugar
1 tablespoon hoisin sauce
120–150ml (4–5fl oz) hot water

1
For the dough, mix together the flour, yeast and sugar in a mixing bowl. Using a spatula or wooden spoon, gradually mix in the measured warm water until all the flour has been incorporated. Add the vegetable oil and then start to knead the dough well with your hands for no more than a minute until smooth.

2
Drizzle a little more oil over the dough, cover the bowl with a damp tea towel and allow to rest and rise in a warm place for 1½ hours.

3
Meanwhile, if making the dipping sauce to serve with the bread as a snack, toast the ½ teaspoon of sesame seeds in a dry wok over a medium heat for 2–3 minutes until fragrant and golden brown, then mix with the other sauce ingredients in a small bowl.

4
For the filling, toast the fennel seeds and Sichuan peppercorns in the wok over a medium heat for about 1 minute until fragrant. Grind into a powder using a pestle and mortar or spice grinder, then mix with the rest of the filling ingredients until a spreadable, paste-like texture is formed.

5
Once the dough has finished resting and rising, lightly oil your work surface and then roll the dough out into a 3–4mm (about ⅛ inch) thick rectangle.

6
Spoon the filling across the dough and spread it out evenly. Roll up the dough from one short side into a log shape, then cut it into 10–12 slices. Lay the slices flat and press down with the palm of your hand into rounds no less than 5mm (¼ inch) thick.

7
Put the 200g (7oz) sesame seeds into a bowl. Dampen both sides of the dough rounds with a little water and then press them into the sesame seeds. Place on a baking tray or plate and allow to rest for another 20 minutes.

8
Heat 1 tablespoon of vegetable oil in a large frying pan over a medium heat, add the dough rounds and fry for 4–5 minutes on each side until golden brown. Serve with the dipping sauce, if you have made it.

GLOSSARY

UK	US
aubergine	eggplant
baking paper	parchment paper
beef shin	beef shank
bicarbonate of soda	baking soda
birds' eye chilli	Thai chili pepper
caster sugar	superfine sugar
chilli flakes	crushed red pepper flakes
Chinese leaf	napa cabbage
choi sum	choy sum
chopping board	cutting board
clingfilm	plastic wrap
cocktail stick	toothpick
coriander	cilantro (if referring to the leaves and stalks/stems)
cornflour	cornstarch
desiccated coconut	dry unsweetened coconut
fan-assisted oven	convection oven
fast-action dried yeast	activea dry yeast
fish slice	spatula
flour, plain	flour, all-purpose
griddle pan	grill pan
grill (in an oven)	broiler/broil (in an oven)
groundnut oil	peanut oil
hob	stove
hor fun rice noodles	flat rice noodles (also called ho fun and chow fun)
jug	liquid measure cup
kai choi	Chinese mustard
kai lan	Also known as Chinese kale
kitchen paper	paper towel
minced meat (e.g. minced pork)	ground meat (e.g. ground pork)
pak choi	bok choy
petit pois	baby garden peas
prawns, king/tiger	shrimp, jumbo
rapeseed oil	canola oil
scallops, king	scallops, jumbo
soda water	club soda
spring onion	scallion
spring roll/wonton pastry	spring roll/wonton wrappers
steak, rump	steak, sirloin
takeaway	takeout
tea towel	dish towel
Tenderstem broccoli	baby broccoli (Broccolini)
tung choi/morning glory	water spinach
wood ear mushrooms	black fungus mushrooms

INDEX

A

American long grain rice 27
asparagus
  scallops & asparagus in Shaoxing rice wine 61
aubergines
  aubergine with spring onion & garlic dressing 112
  seafood-stuffed roast peppers & aubergines 170
  Sichuan-style aubergine 144
  three treasure vegetables 69

B

baguette
  rustic prawn toast 94
balancing flavour, texture & colour 43
bamboo shoots 32
  sweet-&-sour pork strips 74
basmati rice 26
batter
  childhood chicken wings with sticky chilli dip 103
  crispy crispy sweet & sour pork 87
  tempura glazed sea bass 99
beans
  dried yellow soybeans 37
  preserved fermented black beans 38
  salted soybeans 38
beansprouts
  Hong Kong-style fried noodles 65
  Singapore noodles 54
  Yunnan little pot rice noodles 161

beef
  beef brisket noodle soup 150
  Beijing griddled beef 191
  Hunan-style spicy beef 67
  sizzling pepper beef 175
  succulent crispy chilli beef 105
black beans
  black bean beef in beer 68
  black bean skate wing 121
  black bean spare ribs 133
  mapo tofu 66
  preserved fermented black beans 38
braising 141, 143
bread
  Beijing sesame bread 212
breadcrumbs
  panko breadcrumbs 38
  stuffed tofu with soy dressing 113
bream
  crispy bream with pickled red onion & sweet chilli dressing 83
broccoli
  flash-fried venison & broccoli with ginger & spring onion 70
broth. *see* **soup**
butterflying 21

C

cabbage
  flash-fried cabbage with dried chillies & sweetened soy 56
  pickled Tianjin cabbage 37
carrots
  cod fillet with wood ear mushroom & spring onion broth 156
  crispy crispy sweet & sour pork 87
  glass noodle chicken salad 209
  pickled carrot & daikon 203
  three sliver salad 211
cashew nuts
  School of Wok's Sichuan chicken 51
celery
  cod fillet with wood ear mushroom & spring onion broth 156
chestnuts
  yong ping yellow chicken 164
chicken
  charred pineapple chicken in sweetened black rice vinegar 90
  childhood chicken wings with sticky chilli dip 103
  chilli & plum sauce wings 184
  Chongqing chilli chicken 96
  clay-pot chicken & mushroom rice with chilli & garlic sauce 123
  five spice lotus leaf chicken with Chinese sausage 132
  glass noodle chicken salad 209
  Hainanese chicken rice with ginger oil 158
  School of Wok's Sichuan chicken 51
  Singaporean chicken in ginger & garlic paste 137
  soy sauce chicken 147
  yong ping yellow chicken 164
chilli bean sauce 30
  trout with chilli bean, garlic & ginger oil 128
chilli garlic sauce 35
chilli powder 33
chilli sauce/paste
  childhood chicken wings with sticky chilli dip 103
  river shrimp with homemade chilli sauce 120

chillies
 chilli & garlic 'wealthy' clams 60
 chilli & plum sauce wings 184
 Chongqing chilli chicken 96
 clay-pot chicken & mushroom rice with chilli & garlic sauce 123
 crispy crispy sweet & sour pork 87
 double-cooked green beans with chilli hoisin 179
 dried red chillies 33
 flash-fried cabbage with dried chillies & sweetened soy 56
 flash-fried morning glory 198
 fresh hot pot chilli & garlic oil 41
 Hainanese chicken rice with ginger oil 158
 Hunan-style spicy beef 67
 Northern Chinese roast lamb ribs 178
 pickled potato 207
 river shrimp with homemade chilli sauce 120
 salmon bites in xo onion sauce 63
 salt & pepper chilli squid 92
 salted egg prawns 98
 School of Wok's Sichuan chicken 51
 sea bass with crushed soy beans & chilli sauce 122
 Sichuan boiled fish 160
 Sichuan pepper chilli oil 41
 succulent crispy chilli beef 105
 tempura glazed sea bass 99
 twice-cooked chilli pork 182
 twice-cooked squid with garlic & green chilli 176
 wontons in chilli broth 124–5
 yong ping yellow chicken 164
chin kiang rice vinegar 35
Chinese broccoli 197
 flash-fried venison & broccoli with ginger & spring onion 70
Chinese five spice 33
Chinese greens 196–7
 beef brisket noodle soup 150
 glazed Chinese greens with oyster sauce 202

Chinese leaf
 grandma's 'lionhead' meatballs 153
 hoisin duck spring rolls 84–6
 shiitake & chive dumplings 82
 wontons in chilli broth 124–5
chiu chow chilli oil 35
chives
 shiitake & chive dumplings 82
 wontons in chilli broth 124–5
choi sum 197
 beef brisket noodle soup 150
 glazed Chinese greens with oyster sauce 202
choppers 10
chopsticks for cooking 16
cinnamon sticks 39
clams
 chilli & garlic 'wealthy' clams 60
cleavers 10
 meat slicing 20–1
 slicing & dicing 19
 'the crab' technique 18
cloud ear fungus
 dried shredded cloud ear fungus 38
 sweet-&-sour pork strips 74
cloves 39
coconut
 crispy prawns with coconut shallot crunch 100
 desiccated coconut 38
cod
 cod fillet with wood ear mushroom & spring onion broth 156
 seafood-stuffed roast peppers & aubergines 170
cola
 barbecued hoisin & cola ribs 183
corn oil 28
cornflour 33
crab
 grandma's 'lionhead' meatballs 153
cucumber
 crispy duck breast with pancakes & cucumber pickle 188
 glass noodle chicken salad 209
cumin seeds 39
curried squid 148

D

daikon
 beef brisket noodle soup 150
 pickled carrot & daikon 203
deep-frying 79–81
dicing 19
dipping sauce
 childhood chicken wings with sticky chilli dip 103
double cooking 169
duck
 Cantonese roast duck legs 171
 crispy duck breast with pancakes & cucumber pickle 188
 hoisin duck spring rolls 84–6
dumplings
 scallop siu mai 117
 shiitake & chive dumplings 82
 wontons in chilli broth 124–5

E

edamame beans
 prawn, edamame & pine nut lettuce wraps 58
eggs
 egg-fried rice 50
 pork belly in fermented tofu 154
 salted duck eggs 37
 salted egg prawns 98
 shredded pork wraps 72
equipment 16
 choppers 10
 cleavers 10
 steamers 16
 woks 11, 14–15, 16
evaporated milk 37

F

fennel seeds 38
fish
 cod fillet with wood ear mushroom & spring onion broth 156

INDEX

crispy bream with pickled
 red onion & sweet
 chilli dressing 83
fish with ginger
 & spring onion 130
salmon bites in xo onion
 sauce 63
sea bass with crushed soy
 beans & chilli sauce 122
Sichuan boiled fish 160
tempura glazed sea bass 99
trout with chilli bean, garlic
 & ginger oil 128
flavour, infusing into meat 21
fungus
 dried shredded cloud
  ear fungus 38
 sweet-&-sour pork strips 74

G

garlic
 aubergine with spring onion
  & garlic dressing 112
 chilli & garlic 'wealthy' clams 60
 clay-pot chicken
  & mushroom rice with
  chilli & garlic sauce 123
 flash-fried morning glory 198
 fresh hot pot chilli
  & garlic oil 41
 garlic skin oil 41
 scallops with garlic
  & vermicelli 117
 Singaporean chicken in ginger
  & garlic paste 137
 stir-fried pea shoots
  with garlic 199
 trout with chilli bean, garlic
  & ginger oil 128
 twice-cooked squid with
  garlic & green chilli 176
garlic skin oil 41
ginger
 fish with ginger & spring
  onion 130
 flash-fried venison & broccoli
  with ginger & spring onion 70
 ginger & spring onion oil 41
 Hainanese chicken rice with
  ginger oil 158
 Singaporean chicken in ginger
  & garlic paste 137

trout with chilli bean, garlic
 & ginger oil 128
glutinous rice 27
green beans
 double-cooked green beans
  with chilli hoisin 179
greens. *see* **Chinese greens**
groundnut oil 28

H

hoisin sauce 30

I

ingredients 23

J

K

kai choi 196
 mustard greens
  & pak choi salad 208
 Sichuan boiled fish 160
 Yunnan little pot rice
  noodles 161
kai lan 197
 flash-fried morning glory 198
kecap manis 35
kelp
 three sliver salad 211

L

ladles 16
lamb
 Northern Chinese roast
  lamb ribs 178

 lettuce
 prawn, edamame & pine nut
  lettuce wraps 58
lotus leaves
 five spice lotus leaf chicken
  with Chinese sausage 132
lotus roots
 five spice lotus leaf chicken
  with Chinese sausage 132
 pickled lotus root & spinach 206

M

mandarin peel 39
meat
 butterflying 21
 infusing flavour into 21
 slicing techniques 20
meatballs
 grandma's 'lionhead'
  meatballs 153
milk
 evaporated milk 37
morning glory 196
 flash-fried morning
  glory 198
mushrooms
 clay-pot chicken
  & mushroom rice with
  chilli & garlic sauce 123
 cod fillet with wood ear
  mushroom & spring
  onion broth 156
 dried golden lily
  mushrooms 36
 dried shiitake mushrooms 32
 five spice lotus leaf chicken
  with Chinese sausage 132
 Hong Kong-style fried
  noodles 65
 mixed mushroom
  & tofu stew 146
 pak choi with Chinese
  mushroom sauce 64
 scallop siu mai 117
 shiitake & chive
  dumplings 82
 stuffed tofu with soy
  dressing 113
 Taiwanese braised
  pork rice 157
 wontons in chilli
  broth 124–5

mustard greens
    mustard greens & pak choi salad 208
    Sichuan boiled fish 160
    Yunnan little pot rice noodles 161

N

noodles 24–5
    beef brisket noodle soup 150
    glass noodle chicken salad 209
    Hong Kong-style fried noodles 65
    scallops with garlic & vermicelli 117
    shiitake & chive dumplings 82
    Singapore noodles 54
    Yunnan little pot rice noodles 161

O

oils 28–9, 41
onions
    crispy bream with pickled red onion & sweet chilli dressing 83
    crispy fried onions 33
    crispy prawns with coconut shallot crunch 100
    salmon bites in xo onion sauce 63
    three treasure vegetables 69
organisation 17, 48
    balancing flavour, texture & colour 43
    the 'wok clock' 42
oyster sauce 30
    glazed Chinese greens with oyster sauce 202

P

pak choi 197
    beef brisket noodle soup 150
    Hong Kong-style fried noodles 65
    mustard greens & pak choi salad 208
    pak choi with Chinese mushroom sauce 64
    pickled pak choi 36
    shiitake & chive dumplings 82
pancakes
    crispy duck breast with pancakes & cucumber pickle 188
    shredded pork wraps 72
pea shoots
    stir-fried pea shoots with garlic 199
peppercorns
    Sichuan pepper chilli oil 41
    Sichuan peppercorns 39
    sizzling pepper beef 175
peppers
    black bean beef in beer 68
    black pepper tofu 75
    charred pineapple chicken in sweetened black rice vinegar 90
    classic sweet & sour pork 91
    hoisin duck spring rolls 84–6
    School of Wok's Sichuan chicken 51
    seafood-stuffed roast peppers & aubergines 170
    Singapore noodles 54
    three treasure vegetables 69
petit pois
    egg-fried rice 50
pickles 195
    crispy bream with pickled red onion & sweet chilli dressing 83
    crispy duck breast with pancakes & cucumber pickle 188
    pickled carrot & daikon 203
    pickled lotus root & spinach 206
    pickled pak choi 36
    pickled potato 207
    pickled Tianjin cabbage 37
pine nuts
    prawn, edamame & pine nut lettuce wraps 58
pineapple
    charred pineapple chicken in sweetened black rice vinegar 90
plum sauce 34
    chilli & plum sauce wings 184
poaching 141–2

pork
    black bean spare ribs 133
    classic sweet & sour pork 91
    crispy crispy sweet & sour pork 87
    crispy pork belly 174
    grandma's 'lionhead' meatballs 153
    Kampo's pork belly & sweet potato with hoisin spring onion sauce 134
    mapo tofu 66
    pork belly in fermented tofu 154
    scallop siu mai 117
    shredded pork wraps 72
    sweet-&-sour pork strips 74
    Taiwanese braised pork rice 157
    twice-cooked chilli pork 182
potatoes
    pickled potato 207
    three treasure vegetables 69
prawns
    crispy prawns with coconut shallot crunch 100
    grandma's 'lionhead' meatballs 153
    prawn, edamame & pine nut lettuce wraps 58
    river shrimp with homemade chilli sauce 120
    rustic prawn toast 94
    salted egg prawns 98
    scallop siu mai 117
    seafood-stuffed roast peppers & aubergines 170
    Singapore noodles 54
    super-crispy twice-fried prawns in sweet soy 189
    wontons in chilli broth 124–5
preparation 17
    the 'wok clock' 42

R

rapeseed oil 28
red rice vinegar 34
rice 26–7
    boiled/steamed 27
    Cantonese roast duck legs 171
    clay-pot chicken & mushroom rice with chilli & garlic sauce 123
    egg-fried rice 50

Hainanese chicken rice
with ginger oil 158
Taiwanese braised pork rice 157
rice bran oil 29
rice vinegar 31
roasting 169

S

salads
glass noodle chicken
salad 209
mustard greens & pak choi
salad 208
three sliver salad 211
salmon
salmon bites in xo onion
sauce 63
salt & pepper chilli squid 92
sambal sauce 35
sauces 30–1, 34–5
sausages
five spice lotus leaf chicken
with Chinese sausage 132
scallops
scallop siu mai 116
scallops & asparagus
in Shaoxing rice wine 61
scallops with garlic
& vermicelli 117
sea bass
fish with ginger & spring
onion 130
sea bass with crushed soy
beans & chilli sauce 122
Sichuan boiled fish 160
tempura glazed sea bass 99
seafood
chilli & garlic 'wealthy' clams 60
crispy prawns with coconut
shallot crunch 100
curried squid 148
grandma's 'lionhead'
meatballs 153
prawn, edamame & pine nut
lettuce wraps 58
river shrimp with homemade
chilli sauce 120
rustic prawn toast 94
salt & pepper chilli
squid 92
salted egg prawns 98
scallop siu mai 116

scallops & asparagus
in Shaoxing rice wine 61
scallops with garlic
& vermicelli 117
seafood-stuffed roast
peppers & aubergines 170
Singapore noodles 54
super-crispy twice-fried
prawns in sweet soy 189
wontons in chilli broth 124–5
seaweed
three sliver salad 211
sesame oil 29, 31
sesame paste 34
Beijing sesame bread 212
sesame seeds 33
Beijing sesame bread 212
black sesame seeds 37
charred pineapple chicken
in sweetened black rice
vinegar 90
Shaoxing rice wine 34
scallops & asparagus
in Shaoxing rice wine 61
shrimp. *see* **prawns**
Sichuan peppercorns
Chongqing chilli chicken 96
skate
black bean skate wing 121
slices 16
slicing 19
meat 20–1
soup
beef brisket noodle soup 150
cod fillet with wood ear
mushroom & spring
onion broth 156
soy sauce 31
kecap manis 35
soy sauce chicken 147
super-crispy twice-fried
prawns in sweet soy 189
soybeans
dried yellow soybeans 37
salted soybeans 38
sea bass with crushed soy
beans & chilli sauce 122
spare ribs
barbecued hoisin
& cola ribs 183
black bean spare ribs 133
spatulas 16
spices 33
spinach
pickled lotus root
& spinach 206

spring onions
aubergine with spring onion
& garlic dressing 112
Beijing griddled beef 191
cod fillet with wood ear
mushroom & spring
onion broth 156
fish with ginger
& spring onion 130
flash-fried venison & broccoli
with ginger & spring onion 70
ginger & spring onion oil 41
Kampo's pork belly & sweet
potato with hoisin spring
onion sauce 134
spring rolls
hoisin duck spring rolls 84–6
squid
curried squid 148
salt & pepper chilli squid 92
twice-cooked squid with
garlic & green chilli 176
sriracha chilli sauce 35
star anise 39
steak
Beijing griddled beef 191
black bean beef in beer 68
succulent crispy chilli beef 105
steamers 16, 110
steaming 109–11
stir-frying 11, 47–9
strainers 16
sweet & sour sauce
classic sweet & sour pork 91
crispy crispy sweet
& sour pork 87
sweet chilli sauce 35
sweet potatoes
Kampo's pork belly & sweet
potato with hoisin spring
onion sauce 134

T

tamarind concentrate 37
techniques
balancing flavour, texture
& colour 43
braising 141, 143
cleaver skills 18
deep-frying 79–81
dicing 19
poaching 141–2

preparation 17
roasting & double cooking 169
slicing 19
steaming 109–11
stir-frying 11, 47–9
the 'wok clock' 42
tempura glazed sea bass 99
tofu
black pepper tofu 75
mapo tofu 66
mixed mushroom
  & tofu stew 146
pork belly in fermented
  tofu 154
red fermented tofu 36
silken tofu 37
stuffed tofu with soy
  dressing 113
three sliver salad 211
tomatoes
flash-fried cabbage
  with dried chillies
  & sweetened soy 56
**trout with chilli bean, garlic
  & ginger oil 128**
tung choi 196
flash-fried morning
  glory 198

U

utensils 16

V

vegetable oil 28
vegetables
Chinese greens 196–7
three treasure vegetables 69
venison
flash-fried venison
  & broccoli with ginger
  & spring onion 70
vermicelli
scallops with garlic
  & vermicelli 117

W

water chestnuts 32
grandma's 'lionhead'
  meatballs 153
***wok hei* 47**
woks 11
lids for 16
seasoning & maintaining 14–15
'wok air' 47
wontons
scallop siu mai 116
wontons in chilli broth 124–7

X

XO sauce 35

Y

yellow bean paste 34

ACKNOWLEDGEMENTS

To my wife and kids; your crazy loving chaos always keeps me going. Dee, I love that after 15 years of non-stop smoky cooking with minimal extraction, you still allow me back in the house with my clothes smelling of sesame oil and fish sauce. A special dedication to Theo for quietly guessing what I have cooked once I'm home lying next to you at bedtime, and to my little sous chef Rosa for allowing me to build your 'bridges' out of dining chairs whilst cooking dinners with me – you both provide me with such moments of joy.

To my mum and sisters for sharing your love of pig skin and chicken bones with me, and to my late father for the continued inspiration from afar. Somehow, somewhere up there your innate cheekiness and random philosophies help me plough on. All the delicious memories motivate me to keep writing about food in my own way. Also, in loving memory of my late sister-in-law, Deepa, and to the rest of the family for continuing to devour my sambal and satay sauce without breathing in between.

The Octopus Hamlyn team, Natalie Bradley, Kate Fox, Jaz Bahra, Pauline Bache, Nicky Collings, Constance Lam, Pete Hunt and the wider team who make everything else tick, thanks for continuing to believe in my work, helping to shape the creative content with new designs and add to our growing collection of beautiful books.

To the creative geniuses Kris Kirkham (photographer), Phoebe Pearson (photographer assistant), Meg Jansz (food stylist) and Morag Farquhar (prop stylist) for pulling together something completely new from something quite old. Rewriting a book is much harder than I expected, and you have once again brought such a wealth of creative thinking together to give the whole book a unique and refreshing look.

To Stefan Lind, Nev Leaning and the School of Wok team, if we were a band, this would be a comeback tour named 'the Return of the Lind'. Our original cookery school manager jumped back into managing the school and straight into the new iteration of *Chinese Unchopped* as if he'd never been away: amazing work and massively appreciated.

To my Curious Crab Productions gang – Clare Cassidy Sefati, Chris Jackson and Lee Skillett – for holding the fort while on I was shoots, and generally letting me do my thing!

To Freya Deabill of The Brand New Studio, for another epic list of wok clocks, illustrations and help with the front cover! Your work really does 'wok our world'.

To Adrienne Katz Kennedy for helping create the base and history of this book from the original prose.

And lastly to my agent, Richard Watts whose energy and excitement around everything we do surpasses my own. You are not just an agent, but a true friend and long-term business partner who takes the time to understand my vision and expertise, and helps me deliver this with utmost integrity. We are a dream team and you know it!

hamlyn

Published in Great Britain in 2026
by Hamlyn, an imprint of
Octopus Publishing Group Ltd

Carmelite House
50 Victoria Embankment
London EC4Y 0DZ
www.octopusbooks.co.uk

An Hachette UK Company
www.hachette.co.uk

The authorized representative in the EEA is Hachette Ireland, 8 Castlecourt Centre, Dublin 15, D15 XTP3, Ireland (email: info@hbgi.ie)

Text copyright © Jeremy Pang 2026
Design and layout copyright
© Octopus Publishing Group 2026

Distributed in the US by
Hachette Book Group
1290 Avenue of the Americas
4th and 5th Floors
New York, NY 10104

Distributed in Canada by
Canadian Manda Group
664 Annette St.
Toronto, Ontario, Canada M6S 2C8

All rights reserved. No part of this work may be reproduced or utilized in any form or by any means, electronic or mechanical, including photocopying, recording or by any information storage and retrieval system, without the prior written permission of the publisher.

Jeremy Pang has asserted his right under the Copyright, Designs and Patents Act 1988 to be identified as the author of this work.

ISBN (UK): 978-0-60063-991-6
ISBN (US): 978-0-60063-813-1

A CIP catalogue record for this book is available from the British Library.

Printed and bound in Malaysia.

1 3 5 7 9 10 8 6 4 2

Some recipes in this book have previously been published in *Chinese Unchopped: Authentic Chinese recipes broken down into simple techniques*

EDITORIAL DIRECTOR Natalie Bradley
PUBLISHER Kate Fox
SENIOR EDITOR Pauline Bache
ART DIRECTORS Nicky Collings and Jaz Bahra
SENIOR PRODUCTION MANAGER Peter Hunt

CONSULTANT EDITOR Adrienne Katz Kennedy
DESIGNER Evi-O.Studio | Susan Le, Katherine Zhang & Doreen Zheng
ILLUSTRATOR Freya Deabill
PHOTOGRAPHER Kris Kirkham
FOOD STYLISTS Meg Jansz & Stefan Lind
PROPS STYLIST Morag Farquhar
COPY EDITOR Jo Richardson

COOK'S NOTES

Standard level spoon measurements are used in all recipes.

1 tablespoon = one 15ml spoon

1 teaspoon = one 5ml spoon

Both imperial and metric measurements have been given in all recipes. Use one set of measurements only and not a mixture of both.

Fresh herbs should be used unless otherwise stated. If unavailable, use dried herbs as an alternative but halve the quantities stated.

Oven temperatures are for fan ovens. To adjust for a conventional oven, increase the temperature by 20°C (70°F).

This book includes dishes made with nuts and nut derivatives. It is advisable for customers with known allergic reactions to nuts and nut derivatives and those who may be potentially vulnerable to these allergies, such as babies and children with a family history of allergies, to avoid dishes made with nuts and nut oils. It is also prudent to check the labels of pre-prepared ingredients for the possible inclusion of nut derivatives.

All serving sizes are for a full meal unless otherwise stated. When building several dishes together into a feast please reconsider serving sizes according to how many dishes you are cooking.